# STATISTICS FOR
# PUBLIC ADMINISTRATION

## Practical Uses for
## Better Decision Making

### Second Edition

**Maureen Berner**

## Recent Titles from ICMA Press

**Green Books—Authoritative source books on local government management**

Emergency Management: Principles and Practice for Local Government, 2nd edition
Local Government Police Management, 4th edition
Local Planning: Contemporary Principles and Practice
Management Policies in Local Government Finance, 6th edition
Managing Fire and Emergency Services

**Other recent titles**

Capital Budgeting and Finance: A Guide for Local Governments, 2nd edition
Citizen Surveys for Local Government: A Comprehensive Guide to Making Them Matter
Economic Development: Strategies for State and Local Practice, 2nd edition
The Effective Local Government Manager, 3rd edition
Effective Supervisory Practices, 4th edition
Homeland Security: Best Practices for Local Government, 2nd edition
Human Resource Management in Local Government: An Essential Guide, 3rd edition
Leading Performance Management in Local Government
Leading Your Community: A Guide for Local Elected Leaders
Managing Local Government: Cases in Effectiveness
Managing Local Government Services: A Practical Guide
Service Contracting: A Local Government Guide, 2nd edition

# STATISTICS FOR PUBLIC ADMINISTRATION

## Practical Uses for Better Decision Making

**Second Edition**

**Maureen Berner**
School of Government
University of North Carolina at Chapel Hill

**ICMA** PRESS

ICMA
*Leaders at the Core of Better Communities*

ICMA advances professional local government worldwide. Its mission is to create excellence in local governance by developing and advancing professional management of local government. ICMA, the International City/County Management Association, provides member support; publications, data, and information; peer and results-oriented assistance; and training and professional development to more than 9,000 city, town, and county experts and other individuals and organizations throughout the world. The management decisions made by ICMA's members affect 185 million individuals living in thousands of communities, from small villages and towns to large metropolitan areas.

Library of Congress Cataloging-in-Publication Data

Berner, Maureen.
 Statistics for public administration : practical uses for better decision making / Maureen Berner, School of Government, University of North Carolina at Chapel Hill. -- [Second edition].
    pages cm
  ISBN 978-0-87326-771-7 (softcover : alk. paper) -- ISBN 0-87326-771-0 (softcover : alk. paper) -- ISBN 978-0-87326-776-2 (ebook) -- ISBN 0-87326-776-1 (ebook)  1.  Public administration--Statistical methods.  I. Title.
  JA71.7.B67 2013
  519.5024'351--dc23
                          2012046656

Design and layout: Charles Mountain

Printed in the United States of America
2019   2018
5

## About the Author

Maureen Berner, professor of public administration and government, first joined the University of North Carolina (UNC) School of Government in 1998, teaching program evaluation, statistics, and budgeting. Between 2003 and 2005, she directed efforts at the University of Northern Iowa to provide new outreach activities for local governments based on the UNC model. In 2005, she returned to teaching and writing for MPA students and public officials at the School of Government. She has been active in research and teaching in both academia and government, and her publications include numerous books, book chapters, and journal articles. After earning her master's degree in public policy from Georgetown University in 1991, she worked for four years with the Budget Issues Group at the U.S. General Accounting Office, including a rotation to the U.S. House of Representatives Budget Committee, while serving as a presidential management intern. Berner received her doctorate in public policy from the LBJ School of Public Affairs, University of Texas at Austin.

# Contents

# Preface

To be successful, public administrators need to be able to analyze and evaluate policies, and to understand analyses and evaluations done by others. They need to have some understanding of statistics. I am pleased to team up with ICMA in providing the best basic applied statistics book available to local government managers and students hoping to make their career in the finest profession for people interested in leading *their* communities. The first edition of this book was designed to provide local government officials with the tools necessary to design analyses; gather, analyze, and interpret information; present results; and make recommendations. This second edition has a number of new features that make it easier to read, find the exact information you're seeking, and understand concepts through a multitude of new examples. This edition emphasizes using real public safety (police and fire department) data on issues important to all local governments. A full index helps readers go straight to the topic they need quickly. A new glossary supports the text definitions with easy-to-understand, matter-of-fact explanations. It has been roadtested with real students and real practitioners.

*Statistics for Public Administration: Practical Uses for Better Decision Making*, 2nd ed., is a book on research design and basic applied statistics. However, its primary purpose is not to help public managers master statistical theory; rather, it's to demonstrate how statistics can help them do their jobs better. At the same time, a minimal understanding and appreciation of statistical theory is necessary to use data correctly. My overall goal is to make public administrators educated consumers of statistical information.

Statistics is a language. A secondary goal of this book is to make public administrators effective translators. That is, a public employee needs to be able to communicate information to the appropriate audience, be it a local government manager, the city council, the board of trustees, the board of commissioners, a department head, or the public. After reading this book, you should be able to

- Understand and describe general approaches to and problems with public sector research and data measurement
- Conduct basic statistical analyses of raw data
- Evaluate statistical research performed by others.

The book follows the same general order as the first edition. It progresses through roughly four stages. First, I introduce what I mean by "research." What does it mean to "do" research? How do you recognize research that is well done as opposed to poor or weak research?

Next, I cover the basic use of numbers: how to analyze data using descriptive statistics. What does data look like? The reader will understand the importance of getting a feel for the data in order to assess their usefulness. What kind of data is used in statistical research? How can you differentiate between good and bad data? How can data be manipulated? What are the most common ways to summarize and present data? What do the most common statistics tell us about our data? More importantly, what can our data tell us about our issue (can't forget about that!)? What can't our data tell us?

Third, I show how to use data to draw conclusions and test for relationships. For example, is one thing, such as marketing, related to something else, such as the use of a recycling program? How can probability be useful to managers? How can probability be used to assess risk? How can managers tell when something unusual has occurred? How do you move from merely describing a situation to evaluating it? How can you test an idea and be confident of your conclusions?

Finally, I introduce the principles of regression analysis, the most common of the more sophisticated social science research tools, and one that is used in the work of analysts in budget and management offices of major departments or the city manager's office in larger jurisdictions. Regression helps us understand how things are related. Is the relationship strong or weak, major or minor? Can we actually say something is causing something else? How does regression work? Why is it so popular in program analysis? What are its weaknesses and strengths? How does one interpret research using regression? Is it a useful tool for managers?

Throughout this book, I use the story of Chuck Edwards, the manager of Council Top, Iowa, to illustrate how a manager can use statistics in working through common local government problems. His assistant, Nina, helps quite a bit. She uses basic software programs, such as a spreadsheet program like Microsoft Excel, to do most of her work. Most data analysis can be done with spreadsheet programs. Even basic regression can be done with some special add-ons to standard spreadsheet programs. More advanced work, particularly multivariate regression, should be done with a specialized statistical program. Common statistical packages include SPSS, Stata, and SAS. However, these packages are relatively expensive and very powerful, and they can be overwhelming to a casual user, so I do not recommend that a local government purchase them unless it has devoted and trained staff to work on them regularly as well as a substantial amount of statistical work to be done.

I hesitate to mention many additional resources since they change so often, and any list I provide now will be quickly outdated. However, several resources have stood the test of time and should still be available when you are reading this. First, at the expense of being self-promoting, if you wish to understand more about research methods in general, I suggest *Research Methods of Public Administrators* (2002), a book I coauthored with Elizabethann O'Sullivan and Gary Rassel. For more on the mathematical background of statistics, I suggest consulting *Applied Statistics for Public Administration,* 7th ed. (2008) by Kenneth J. Meier, Jeffrey L. Brudney, and John Bohte. The classic minitext on regression analysis, and the one I always use as a supplement to other texts, is *Applied Regression: An Introduction* (1980), by Michael S. Lewis-Beck. The U.S. Government Accountability Office (GAO) has a number of excellent and accessible publications that provide information on various research methods, quantitative and qualitative, that can be used in program evaluation. I know from experience as a GAO evaluator that every sentence in every publication by GAO is checked and rechecked and checked again by multiple experts against multiple sources.

This book will not train you to use the software or do the actual mathematical calculations; I do not provide an electronic file with data set up in a sample spreadsheet. Nor will this book give you a specific roadmap on how to answer a specific question. No book will do that; that is not how actual life, or management, works. Theory is just theory, not reality. You need to gather real data that are important for a problem facing you. You will really learn how to use statistics only if you need to use them. My goal, again, is to allow local government officials to understand how statistics can help them in their jobs in a real way—to be educated consumers of information.

The town of Council Top is based very loosely on a combination of Traer, Iowa, and Council Bluffs, Iowa, where my husband and I grew up, respectively. I have tremendous respect for the people of Iowa, and I taught some of the smartest, hardest-working, and most ethical undergraduate public administration students at the University of Northern Iowa. I currently have the honor of teaching some of the smartest, hardest-working, and most ethical graduate public administration students at the University of North Carolina at Chapel Hill. I applaud my faculty colleagues here, who are uniformly devoted to providing the best professional public administration training, especially for local government, in the country.

I want to thank the University of North Carolina at Chapel Hill's School of Government for providing incredible support in every aspect of my work. I also want to thank ICMA, devoted to excellence in local government management, for publishing this book. ICMA is invaluable to local government officials in any field in any state. They are the "go-to" source on any local government issue. I encourage all readers of this book, student, teacher or official, to consider active membership in the association. It provides a high return on investment.

The character of Chuck Edwards is loosely based on my oldest brother, whom I love very much (and not to any greater or lesser extent than any of my other four older brothers or older sister!). I want to express my incredible appreciation for Chuck and my brother John in taking care of our mother at this time in our lives, in the course of my writing this book, when she needed it most.

Nina is a really smart, cool, and caring German student. Maria is a really smart, cool, and caring Brazilian student. Rex and Will really do love LEGO® sets. I want to thank my husband, Andy, and my kids, William, Yvette, Maxwell, and, not the least, Leo (who had the wonderful timing of being born in the course of my writing this book). Natalia and Rachel are Leo's Spanish moms. Thank you all for allowing me time to write around taking care of my family, my most important and fun job. I hope the kids always remember the summer of 2012.

# You Have to Answer a Question, So Now What?

## [RESEARCH DESIGN]

**"Chuck, you're crazy.** How are you going to convince the council that this is a good idea?"

Chuck Edwards eased back in his chair. He had been city manager of Council Top for only a year, after serving three years as assistant manager. When he was hired, he found that good people had made most past decisions thoughtfully and with good intentions, but that there was often little or no information to help along the process. Decisions were driven by anecdotes, by complaints from anywhere from one to ten people, or by someone who proposed an idea with which someone else agreed and everyone else went along. With his new position as manager, Chuck knew that he wanted to use information in a better way; he wanted to actually have numbers to back up good proposals, counter proposals that didn't sound quite right, and help him figure out the difference.

The problem was that he wasn't used to using research, and he didn't have the time or energy to take a research course at Western Community College. In fact, he really didn't want to "do" research; he just wanted to have some of his staff work with solid information rather than guesses. Well, that is not completely true. He wanted to be able to understand the numbers himself and then explain them to his council in a way that did not make him look like a complete idiot.

His proposal was to hire a management analyst, someone who would help him increase the city's capacity to crunch numbers. He had just told Joan, the human resource (HR) manager, that he wanted to develop a new position description that he could propose to the council at the next meeting. She was skeptical that it was going to be worth her time.

"Joan, I know the council is against hiring anyone who doesn't do something traditional, like keep the books or clean the streets or save people from burning buildings.
But the city is growing, the decisions are a lot more complicated than they have been
before, and a lot more money is at stake. We need better information and someone
who can understand it. And *we* need to understand it. I don't want to be swamped under a lot of numbers and fancy statistics terms that you need a PhD to decipher. And I
need to be able to explain it to the council in a way that makes decisions easier."

"I still don't think the council will go for it." Joan looked at Chuck over her glasses.

"All I have to do is bring up the fiasco over the planning for the senior center and
remind them of how, having made a bunch of assumptions about who would use it, we
built it completely wrong and just had to spend three million dollars to revamp it. That
cost the last manager her job, and I don't want a repeat. A management analyst will be
a good investment if we can use the information to avoid bad decisions."

"Well, when you bring that up, you might get the votes. I'll get the position description ready before Monday night."

This book is for Chuck, Joan, the new management analyst, the council, and any
other public sector official who wants to use information, primarily numbers,
to make better decisions. It will not make you a statistician or a card-carrying data
nerd. The objective is to make you an educated consumer of statistical information.
That is, you will be able to

- Understand and use statistical information
- Recognize what is involved in research
- Distinguish between good analyses and poor analyses.

When the next consultant delivers a report, you actually will be able to read some
of the chapters rather than just flipping to the conclusion and trusting that the consultant did the analysis correctly.

Throughout the book, you will see certain words in **bold**. Although statisticians
often use these terms, they represent simple concepts. I will introduce the official
term and then explain the concept so that you can untangle "stats talk." In addition,
this edition includes a glossary and an index to help you understand the terms and
locate them throughout the book.

## Developing a good research design

The book is organized to help you understand statistics. Statistics consist of numbers. But numbers don't just fall out of the sky. Before you crunch any data, you
have to be clear exactly what it is that you want to know! In other words, what

information would be helpful to make a decision? What numbers should you collect? How can you get this information? And how can you know if it is any good?

This chapter walks you through the major steps you need to take before you even see your first number. If you can read only one chapter in this book, this is it. The first six steps focus on developing the primary research question, while Steps 7 and 8 introduce the methodology and data considerations necessary to conduct the research. Together, these eight steps represent the research design process:

1. Understand the issue. (Identify the background and context.)
2. Identify the problem. (Write a problem statement.)
3. Explain your theory. (What do you think is going on? What is your theory?)
4. Formulate the research question. (Identify what you need to know to test your theory. What is the general research question?)
5. Formulate the hypothesis. (Specifically identify what you need to know to test your theory. What hypothesis do you want to test?)
6. Operationalize the hypothesis. (Identify exactly what you need to know to test your theory. How do you operationalize your hypothesis?)
7. Select the methodology. (Figure out how you are going to gather that information. Choose your methodology.)
8. Evaluate the data. (Decide if the data you gather are good enough to answer your questions, inform your decision, and help you solve your problem.)

## Walking through the research design process

Why do we place such importance on this preliminary planning work? Simple: garbage in, garbage out. If we do not plan our questions well, it is easy to fall into the trap of gathering data that sit on a shelf or, in this electronic age, in a computer file to be unused and forgotten. Let's walk through these eight steps.

### Step 1: Understand the issue. (Identify the background and context.)

Instead of asking ourselves, "What is the issue?", we often jump into gathering numbers before understanding the background and context. The first step of the research process is to **understand the issue** involved. In Council Top, Iowa, the fictional town that provides the backdrop for this book, the population had been growing as people moved in from the nearby small towns. The manager faced multiple issues that a manager would not have faced twenty years ago: increasing demands for technology, health care, social services, transportation, and housing services, to name a few. In real-life situations, the context would include information not just about a population and the services it needs but also about a sensitive political situation, upcoming elections, budgetary constraints, new state or federal mandates, reforms in related areas such as mental health services or testing in the schools, zoning controversies, public-private partnerships, ethics, etc.

**Step 2: Identify the problem. (Write a problem statement.)**

Once we understand the background and context of the issue, we need to identify the problem. The second step in developing a good research design is writing a problem statement. It can be difficult to develop a single sentence that captures exactly what the problem is, but this step is vital. Have you ever heard of people who have a great solution and are looking for a problem? This is one of the pitfalls of failing to understand the issue and to identify the problem correctly. Identifying the problem justifies why you find it necessary to make a change or need to reach a decision. It is not a means for adopting a "great solution" and fitting it to a problem that may or may not exist. The well-written **problem statement** will state clearly and specifically a situation that is, well, a problem. For example,

- The number of bicycle accidents has increased dramatically over the past five years.
- The public safety budget is already in the red, six months from the end of the fiscal year.
- The complaints from senior citizens indicate that local government services are too hard to access, which could lead to underuse of services, poorer health care, and lower quality of life for the elderly population.
- The streets flood on a higher-than-average basis compared to other local governments in the region; this inconveniences residents and contributes to the deterioration of roads.
- The animal control reports cite over ten cases of rabid raccoons in the area (more than in any previous year), endangering public health and causing reports of panic among suburban parents and pet owners.

Why bother with this step? If you cannot clearly state what the problem is, you cannot focus your research in a way that gets directly to the point. You wander in a wilderness of data, not sure what information will be helpful and what will not. You gather any data available; hoping that somewhere in the numbers is the key information you need. You might try to solve multiple problems at once, or solve the wrong problem, or even assume that there is a problem where there really is not one.

**Step 3: Explain your theory. (What do you think is going on? What is your theory?)**

Now that you have a clear understanding of the issue and have written your problem statement, what do you think is going on? What is your theory about what is causing the problem? The goal of this third step is to explain your theory by outlining how different things or events relate to each other. In statistical terms, we refer to this as **developing a model**. A model is just a diagram of how you think various actors, situations, or other **indicators** relate to each other. A model can be very simplistic or very complex. For example, Figure 1–1 illustrates how a simple model might look:

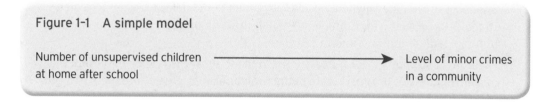

Figure 1-1   A simple model

Number of unsupervised children                          ⟶          Level of minor crimes
at home after school                                                        in a community

In this model, I am theorizing a particular relationship: that the number of unsupervised children at home after school is related to the level of minor crimes in a community. At this point, I am not sure this is the case; I have no evidence, or data, to support this theory. In fact, my model is not complete. Many other things probably influence the level of minor crimes in a community. A more complete model might look like Figure 1–2:

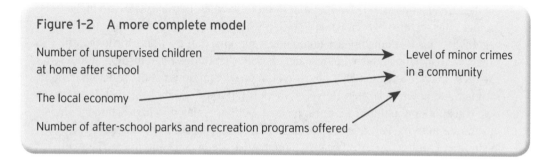

Figure 1-2   A more complete model

Number of unsupervised children                          ⟶          Level of minor crimes
at home after school                                                        in a community

The local economy

Number of after-school parks and recreation programs offered

Just as there are simple and complex relationships, every model will be different depending on the situation and relationships we are trying to describe and outline. Usually our task doesn't involve fully describing a model; we don't need to understand every connection or identify every indicator. We are just interested in a few major relationships that we hope we can influence in our role as a government official.

What counts as a relationship? As we'll discuss in more detail in Chapter 8, a relationship needs four things: time order, theoretical support, co-variation, and legitimacy.

1. **Time order.** What is an appropriate time order between the things or events? In other words, what comes first? For example, if you want to look at the potential link between the poor local economy and the number of minor crimes, the poor economy would happen first, and the increase in minor crimes would follow. An increase in minor crimes would not happen first. When you think about time order, it is also a good idea to think about how much time, reasonably, you expect to see between the two events. Would it take about a year to start seeing an increase in minor crimes after a downturn in the economy? Time order will have

an impact in later steps when we actually gather some data; we want to match up the data correctly, for example, to match the data on the economy in one year with the data on minor crimes a year later.

2. **Theoretical support.** Does the relationship make sense? Is it logical to think that greater numbers of unsupervised children might lead to greater numbers of minor crimes? Is it logical to think that if the local economy is poor, there will be a higher level of minor crimes?

3. **Co-variation.** In a relationship, the two parts of the relationship will move together, either both increasing or both decreasing (showing a **positive relationship,** such as more unsupervised children and more minor crime, as in Figure 1–1) or one increasing while the other decreases (showing a **negative,** or **inverse, relationship,** such as lower economic growth and higher crime, as in Figure 1–2).

4. **Legitimacy.** Researchers are only interested in measuring true relationships. In other words, they hope they are not measuring false, or **spurious,** relationships. For example, researchers have data showing that in months when Popsicle sales are higher, murder rates are also higher. So do Popsicles cause people to murder each other? To begin with, this relationship lacks theoretical support; that is, it fails the logic test. However, it also illustrates what researchers call a "spurious relationship." It looks like there may be a relationship because both go up and down at the same time: up in summer and down in winter. However, there is not a true relationship between Popsicle consumption and murder rates. Instead, both are related to higher temperatures! In summer months, Popsicle consumption increases. Murder rates also tend to go up in summer months, perhaps because more people are outside and interacting with one another. But the two are not related.

### Step 4: Formulate the research question. (Identify what you need to know to test your theory. What is the general research question?)

Once you **identify the problem** you need to address and **explain your theory**, it is easier to think of what you need to know to test your theory. Identify what you need to know, and this becomes your general research question. For example, you will notice that we could answer each of the research questions in Figure 1–3 with information. There is no subjectivity involved. We are not asking questions that begin with "Should the city do…?" or "What is the best way to…?" Those types of questions belong in the realm of opinion, judgment, experience, discussion, and debate. In this book, we focus on using data to answer informational, evidence-based questions.

### Step 5: Formulate the hypothesis. (Specifically identify what you need to know to test your theory. What hypothesis do you want to test?)

The next step is what most practitioners don't do or perhaps they do it in their heads, but don't usually put it down on paper. This step is to create a **hypothesis,** or even **multiple hypotheses,** that you will test with data to help answer the research

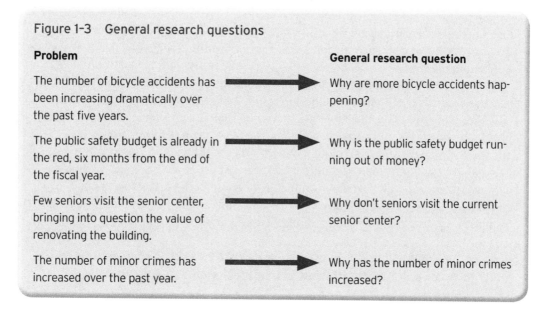

Figure 1-3   General research questions

**Problem**

The number of bicycle accidents has been increasing dramatically over the past five years.

The public safety budget is already in the red, six months from the end of the fiscal year.

Few seniors visit the senior center, bringing into question the value of renovating the building.

The number of minor crimes has increased over the past year.

**General research question**

Why are more bicycle accidents happening?

Why is the public safety budget running out of money?

Why don't seniors visit the current senior center?

Why has the number of minor crimes increased?

question. A hypothesis is nothing more than explicitly stating your hunch or guess. If you state a hypothesis explicitly, it is easier to say, "My guess was right" or "My guess was wrong;" this helps focus your research. Once you have your hypothesis laid out, you will gather data to see if it is true. In research terms, if we find support for our hypothesis, we will probably accept it. If our research does not find support for the hypothesis, we may reject it.

Look at Figure 1–4. Remember that the statements on the right are hypotheses, not statements of fact. We will be testing these statements. If we reject a hypothesis,

Figure 1-4   General research questions and hypotheses

**General research question**

Why are more bicycle accidents happening?

Why is the public safety budget running out of money?

Why don't seniors visit the current senior center?

Why has the number of minor crimes increased?

**General hypothesis**

Recent road construction has made it harder to see bicyclists.

More employees are working overtime than anticipated.

The senior center doesn't offer programs that seniors want.

There are not enough community activities offered to kids after-school.

we might form a new one. For example, if we don't find support for the hypothesis that the senior center doesn't offer programs that seniors want, we might think of a new hypothesis to test, such as that seniors don't visit the center because they cannot get to it easily.

In the course of research, we might focus on testing one specific hypothesis because we have a certain explanation in mind, and once we confirm or reject it, our research is done. However, we might also be searching for an explanation more broadly. In that case, if we reject one hypothesis, we might turn our research to another hypothesis, and then another, and another, until we find support. Alternatively, we might do some exploratory analysis to come up with other possible hypotheses; for example, we may conduct a survey with the seniors with open-ended questions about why they do or do not use the senior center. From their responses, we can then form some more-focused hypotheses to test.

### Step 6: Operationalize the hypothesis. (Identify exactly what you need to know to test your theory. How do you operationalize your hypothesis?)

At some point, we have to stop talking in generalities and be specific. That is, we have to ask a question we can actually answer. When we take something abstract—a hypothesis, for example—and put it into concrete, measurable terms, we **operationalize** it. Ask yourself, "What specific question would let me test my hypothesis, and how can I best phrase it so as to make it the most concrete and measurable?" This is where you identify *exactly* what you need to know to test your theory and hypothesis. In the statements shown in Figure 1–5, we move from our general hypothesis to something with which we can work.

There are many ways to operationalize a general hypothesis. The key is whether we can test and either support or reject it. In research terms, we want the hypothesis to be **falsifiable.** We have to be able, at least theoretically, to disprove it. For example, I could hypothesize that life exists on other planets. However, I cannot disprove that hypothesis. I would have to show that no life exists on any other planet in the universe, and that is impossible (at least at this time).

I would have to visit all the other planets and check for life. So, that cannot be a research hypothesis. Instead, I could form a research hypothesis that there is some form of life, as we know it, on Mars. Whether there is some form of life on Mars is something that we should be able to prove or disprove with current technology; in fact, scientists are trying to do just that.

We have now gone from a problem to a general research question to something we would actually be able measure and test. This is a positive thing! Probably one of the biggest mistakes in research is not spending enough time focusing the research question. But wait! You should make one more consideration. Public administrators are very familiar with the task of gathering data that turn out to be less useful than originally thought. An important point to consider now is whether the specific hypotheses you test will

## Figure 1-5   General and operationalized hypotheses

| General hypothesis | Operationalized hypothesis |
|---|---|
| Recent road construction has made it harder to see bicyclists, causing more accidents. | Areas with road construction have a statistically significant higher incidence of bicycle accidents than areas that do not have road construction. |
| More overtime is being charged than anticipated, causing the budget to go into the red. | The amount of overtime salary actually charged is larger than initially budgeted.<br>*AND*<br>This amount is a significant portion of the amount of overage. |
| The senior center doesn't offer programs that seniors want. | The majority of customer requests for activities in the past year at the senior center have not resulted in planned programs.<br>*OR*<br>The majority of senior citizens disagree with the statement that the senior center offers programs they want. |
| There are not enough community activities offered to kids after school. | The number of community activities offered to children after school has decreased in the past three years.<br>*OR*<br>The majority of parents report that they have no options for after-school activities for their children. |

provide information that decision makers will respect. You can imagine having data to answer the specific, operationalized hypotheses such as the ones on the right in Figure 1–5. If you could confirm or reject those statements, would you be closer to a solution to your problem? If not, you should drop those hypotheses and form others. Don't spend time on gathering data that you will not use.

### Step 7: Select the methodology. (Figure out how you are going to gather that information. Choose your methodology.)

The methods you use to gather the data to test your hypotheses will determine the quality of the overall research. Some problems are so complex that they are very hard to understand despite lots of studies, information, and numbers focused on solving them. The continuing academic achievement gap between two different races is a wonderful example. It will likely take years, maybe decades, for researchers to understand why it persists. For these complex and important "why" questions, different sides may have conflicting data and statistics to back up their findings. Then the debate is not about the numbers but about the quality of the research design and data. There are two main ways that people assess the quality of research: by asking if the **research design** and **research quality** are solid, and by asking if the data are good (which we will discuss in Step 8). First, let's discuss how we select and plan our methodology.

***Research design types.***    Planning how to gather data is the **research design phase**. There are three main designs that we can use to conduct a research project: an experimental design, a quasi-experimental design, or a nonexperimental design. Experimental designs tend to be limited to laboratories, not community centers or housing offices or fire stations. Most public administrators will never work with an experimental design, but it is helpful to understand what it is since it is the benchmark against which all other research is measured.

1. **Experimental designs** have two main characteristics. The first is **control**, as it applies to the setting, the participants, and the experiment's setup. *Control* means everything can be controlled. The researcher can determine all aspects of the setting, such as light, temperature, space, and sound, just like in the cage of a laboratory animal. The researcher can determine exactly who is and who is not in the study, as well as all of their personal characteristics. If the researcher wants only police officers with exactly the same background and history, she can set it up that way. Experimental designs are common in medical or laboratory studies. In a laboratory setting, for example, one set of mice may receive a new drug to prevent cancer while another set, the **control group**, may not. Researchers would then see if the mice in the experimental group develop fewer cases of cancer than those in the control group.

   The second important characteristic is **random assignment.** Regarding how to form these two groups, random assignment means that each person (or mouse, in this example) has an equal chance of placement in the experimental or control group. Why is this valuable? Because any differences between the groups will also be random. There is just as likely to be a fat mouse or a mouse genetically prone to cancer in one group as in the other group. There are no systematic differences between the groups, which mean that there is no **systematic bias** between them. This does not mean that the groups are exactly alike. But there should not be *any pattern* to differences between them other than that due to the experimental drug.

2. Unfortunately, control is not something that public administrators have at their disposal. If we are lucky, we might have a quasi-experimental design. **Quasi-experimental designs** are like they sound. They have one of the two aspects of an experimental design—a control group for comparison or random participation in the groups—but not both. For example, we might be able to start a mentorship program in one school and, after several years, compare student performance in that school to student performance in a school without a mentorship program. By comparing one school with the program to one without, we are using an experimental group and a control group, which meets one of the two criteria for an experimental design. But we can't meet the other criterion: we can't just randomly assign students from the community to the two schools. Therefore, there may be systematic differences between the student bodies in the schools (one may have a higher population of students from single-parent households, for example) that we need to take into account.

3. In a **nonexperimental design,** there is no control group, and participants are not randomly selected. An example of a nonexperimental design would be simply measuring the number of bicycle accidents both before and after implementing a new safety program. Because we didn't control for other things that could have reduced bicycle accidents, such as colder weather, and we didn't select the groups of bikers at random, we don't know for certain if a reduction in accidents was due to our safety program or to something else.

***Research quality.*** In terms of research quality, experimental designs are the strongest. This is why medical research uses them so much. If you are considering prescribing a new treatment for cancer, you want to make sure that the treatment has been tested in the most rigorous way. To be honest, decisions about social problems are just as important, but since there is much less ability to control the situation, quasi-experimental designs are the next preferred approach, with nonexperimental designs coming in last. Unfortunately, public administration managers often have to rely on nonexperimental designs. Their first priority is to manage, not study, and they must deal with changing circumstances constantly. Try as they might, managers often have little control over what happens, to whom, where, and when, day to day throughout the organization.

> The public and researchers alike will have stronger faith in
> the conclusions from a study if the study and its conclusions
> are replicable.

We assess quality of research in two ways: we ask if it is **valid** and we ask if it is **reliable.** These terms have meaning in our normal conversation and have similar, but more specific, meaning in research. For a research design or methodology to be

**valid,** it has to answer the question we want it to answer. That may seem obvious and simplistic, but it is harder to achieve than you might think. The city manager might ask which fire station has the best performance record. Her assistant interprets this as wanting to know which station has the best response time. He could gather data on average response times across stations. Is response time the best way to assess performance? This study may gather important data, but that does not mean it has answered the research question. Or perhaps the study does gather the proper data but from the wrong years or the wrong units, or it mixes up data from good and bad sources, or it has any number of other design or implementation problems. If the study has major flaws in its design or implementation, and it does not really answer the research question, it will not be considered a valid study.

What if there seems to be a solid, well-designed research study on fire station performance, but it was so dependent on the personal observations of the researcher that a different assistant repeating the study got completely different results. For a research design or methodology to be **reliable**, others would have to be able to replicate it and get similar results. This is the second test of a good study. The public and researchers alike will have stronger faith in the conclusions from a study if another person is able to conduct the same study and produce similar results.

### Step 8: Evaluate the data. (Decide if the data you gather are good enough to answer your questions, inform your decision, and help you solve your problem.)

As mentioned in Step 7, we consider experimental designs to be the strongest types of research. That is usually because the level of control we have and our ability to use random assignment to avoid bias mean that we can be more confident in those studies' validity and reliability. But local government officials can't offer a housing program in a laboratory or randomly assign some people to receive food assistance and others to go hungry. Does that mean we shouldn't even try to use data to make decisions? Of course not. Even without a control group or random assignment, we may gather and use quality information. So, how do we know if we have good data?

The qualities of **validity** and **reliability** apply to data, too.

***Validity of data.***    For validity, we ask if our data are really measuring what we want them to measure. Let's say you would like to understand how wealthy your community is. You might simply use U.S. Census Bureau information about average income in different neighborhoods as your data. For most purposes, average income will capture the differences in wealth across neighborhoods very well. Income does not measure assets such as land or stocks, so you would not really be capturing true wealth. On the other hand, financial aid officers at colleges understand how assets like land or a house may represent overall wealth. However, since it is hard to sell a portion of a house or a few acres of farmland to help a child pay for college, these measures of wealth do not represent liquid assets used for the consideration of financial aid. There are many measures of wealth, and it is important to understand exactly what measures you want to use to address the problem at hand.

## Good data measure what you are trying to measure.
## They accurately capture the concept.

Even with measures that you think are valid, you must be careful to make sure that the data are not skewed or mismeasured. For example, in which major at the University of North Carolina will you find graduates who make the highest salary on average? It is not pre-law, pre-med, or business. Surprisingly, it is geography. That is because Michael Jordan, the star basketball player, was a geography major. Figures for average income are often skewed by very high or very low salaries. That is why we use median instead of average (mean) as a more valid measure of income. (More on averages, medians, and other descriptive statistics for evaluating data appears in Chapter 3.) In the end, the concept of *validity* is best associated with the idea of accuracy. Are you measuring what you want to measure?

This is an important concept, so let me provide another example, in keeping with the idea of measuring fire station performance by using response times. Let's say you do think that using response time is a valid way to understand overall station performance. What if one station reports response time as the time from when the 911 call is received to the first truck's arrival at the fire, while another station measures response time as the time from when the first truck leaves the station to its arrival at the fire? This example measures response time in two different ways. Even if the design is valid, the data being gathered are not.

***Reliability of data.***   Reliability with regard to data is similar to reliability with regard to a research design. As discussed, a reliable research design is one that others can replicate. In the same way, reliable data are those that are measured consistently so that if a different researcher makes the same measurement, he or she will obtain the same result.

Let's say we decide that our study of fire station performance should include measurements of how long it takes from when a call needing a response is answered by 911 to when the truck leaves the fire station building (specifically when the back wheel crosses the threshold). An analyst could hang out at the fire station, timing each call using a stopwatch. She comes back the next day but forgot the stopwatch. She uses her regular watch instead. She is sick the following day, so another analyst shows up instead and uses the wall clock. If the wall clock is slow and is adjusted each night by the staff, or the stopwatch is much easier to read than the fashion watch with tiny numbers and no second hand, the data collected will not be reliable. The data would differ based on who was doing the measurement and how). In another example, the same person could time with the same watch, but if that particular watch is always slow, all the results will be incorrect, even if they were measured to the tenth of a second in exactly the same way. With data, the concept of *reliability* is best associated with precision and consistency.

To understand how reliability and validity work together, we can use the analogy of shooting at a target. Someone who shoots in a "valid" way will have all her shots hit the target near the bull's eye. Someone who shoots "reliably" will have all his shots hit the target in the same area, close together. Ideal data are both valid and reliable. That is, the shots will be both near the bull's eye and closely clustered. You have both the correct measure and you measure it correctly.

## "Chuck, the last candidate to interview is here," said Joan.

"Thank you, Joan," replied Chuck tiredly, looking up from the paltry pile of résumés on his desk. He really couldn't call it a stack. "I am just not sure people understand what we need. These candidates either don't like analysis, can't write or speak to explain the analysis, or think massive spreadsheets are the answer to everything."

"I am not sure I understand what we need," said Joan with a smile. She ushered in a young woman in a business suit holding a faux-leather portfolio and wearing a nervous, friendly expression. She was a recent graduate from the Master of Public Administration (MPA) program at State. Joan introduced them. "This is Nina Schorn. Nina, Chuck Edwards, our manager."

After the usual pleasantries, Chuck got down to business. "I am looking for an analyst who can work with me and the staff in the manager's office. We need someone who can work with gathering, analyzing, and reporting information. Data. Numbers. Maybe several numbers. And we need someone who can explain the analysis to our staff and elected officials."

Chuck expected to see her flinch at this, as did the other two candidates he had interviewed. To his surprise, Nina visibly relaxed. "Well, I enjoy working with numbers. But I would rather not work with a lot of data."

"I don't understand," said Chuck, confused. "The position description clearly says the analyst must be able to work with statistics."

"I don't want to work with 'lots' of data; I want to work with the right data. If you ask the right questions, you only need a few answers to make better decisions," Nina said.

Chuck paused, looked down at her résumé, and then looked up at her with a grin. "I think we will get on very well," said Chuck, pushing the rest of the résumés to the side of his desk.

## Review questions

1. What would be examples of each of the following steps in the research design process?

   a. Understand the issue

   b. Identify the problem

   c. Explain your theory

   d. Formulate the research question

   e. Formulate the hypothesis

   f. Operationalize the hypothesis

   g. Select the methodology

   h. Evaluate the data

2. Compose a problem statement that describes something going on in your jurisdiction.

3. Define and give examples of a positive relationship and a negative relationship.

4. Develop a general research question based on the problem statement from Question 2.

5. Develop a hypothesis from each of these general research questions about Council Top, Iowa:

   a. Why are test scores decreasing?

   b. Why has unemployment risen in the past five years?

   c. Why are energy costs rising?

   d. Why have crime rates fallen?

6. Take each hypothesis from Question 5 and describe how you could falsify it.

7. If you were going to conduct research on decreasing test scores, how would you go about using an experimental design?

8. Would an experiment with a control group that has not been randomly assigned be experimental, quasi-experimental, or nonexperimental? Why?

9. A scale in a doctor's office always adds five pounds to people who step on it. Is this scale valid? Is it reliable? Why or why not?

10. Can a researcher have a valid study but not have valid data? How about valid data but not a valid study?

# Muck Around in the Numbers!

## 2

[DESCRIPTIVE STATISTICS]

**Chuck stood at his desk at 6:40 p.m.,** printing off just one more document. The council meeting was starting in twenty minutes, and Chuck had a bad habit of waiting until the last minute before deciding he needed this document or that report handy just in case a council member asked a question he couldn't answer. Nina stopped by his door.

"Are you walking down?" she asked.

Chuck didn't want it to appear that he was scrambling at the last minute, so he ignored the appendixes to the planning report he was printing out. "Sure. Be right with you." I don't really need those appendixes, he thought. No one is going to ask about average parking space sizes in Council Top.

"Are you ready for your first report to the council?" asked Chuck.

"I think so. I wasn't able to gather all the data the council asked for, and I think it will be surprised why," said Nina, walking quickly.

Chuck lengthened his stride to catch up. His staff was getting younger and faster, or he was getting older and slower. He preferred to think it was the former.

This chapter is about the basics of **data**: what data are, what types of data there are, what levels of data there are, and what kinds of data there are. (And, by the way, the word *data* is always plural. A single piece of data is a datum; many pieces are data.) You might ask: aren't data just numbers? No. Data are pieces of information, any kind of information. Some are numbers; some are not. We call each piece of information an **observation**. If you are going to gather data—pieces of information—from fifteen people, you will gather fifteen observations. With more observations, you have more information. We will speak to this point again later, but just as it is always wise to have as much information as possible when making decisions, the same rule applies with statistics. In general, the more observations, the better. (At some point, more information can actually muddy the waters, but we will discuss that in more detail toward the end of the book.)

Remember: the goal of this entire process is to answer a question, the one that you identified in the previous chapter. We need information to answer that question. For example, your county commissioners may want to know if roads in the county are being kept free of trash. You can answer that question in a variety of ways. Typically, a county employee might respond by citing the amount of trash picked up over the previous six months, one measure that the roadways have been cleaned. But that doesn't mean that for every pound of trash picked up, another two weren't dropped. Another way to respond would be to cite the number of miles of roadway that have been "adopted" by community groups, or the number of groups or the total membership of groups that have adopted roadways (assuming that those groups are picking up the trash as expected!). Yet another way would be to cite the number of county employee hours devoted to trash pickup or the amount of dollars allocated to contractors to clean roadways, although again, effort does not mean results.

All these ways involve numbers, which is how we usually think of data. However, what if a county employee presented a video report highlighting the worst areas for littering and showed them both before and after county pickup efforts? Alternatively, citizens who were given free disposable cameras photographed any major trash they encountered on their daily commutes to prepare a photo report. These observations are also data.

<blockquote>
Data are not just numbers; data are pieces of information.
Names, colors, photos, and sounds can all be data.
</blockquote>

Don't limit yourself to starting with numbers. Be creative. You should think about the best way to communicate your information, regardless of the form. Remember, too, that researchers are much more likely to use traditional forms of data in the work that you are likely to encounter.

## Types of data

There are three main types of traditional data: nominal, ordinal, and interval.

### Nominal data

**Nominal data** are data made up of named things (the Latin root of "nominal" is *name*). Another term for nominal data is **categorical data.** This is easy to remember if you think of the data as coming from categories. We will use the more common term, nominal, from this point on. As you can see in Table 2–1, nominal data consist of items that do not have a value attached to them; they are things that are not numbers.

One piece of nominal data cannot be greater or lesser, better or poorer, than any other piece. There is no value attached to a palm tree over an oak. They are simply different.

As we discuss shortly, analyzing nominal data is similar to putting different observations into different boxes and then seeing what patterns emerge. The numbers in the categories may be fewer or greater; you might have more retired neighbors than employed neighbors. But retired is not "better" than employed (at least not in theory). As you will see later, with some types of statistical analysis we may code different categories with a 1 or a 0, but that is only to allow the computer to read our data, not to apply values to them. Statisticians refer to this coding as *creating a dummy variable* because the values of 1 or 0 are "dummies" representing the different categories.

**Table 2-1   Examples of nominal data**

| Variable | Data |
| --- | --- |
| HIV status | Positive, negative |
| Tree species | Oak, maple, birch, palm |
| Sex | Female, male |
| Nationality | Canadian, American, Mexican, Brazilian |
| Zoning | Commercial, residential, industrial |
| Employment status | Employed, unemployed, retired |

## Ordinal data

The next type of data is ordinal. **Ordinal data** also consist of names, or categories, but as you can see in Table 2–2, we can rank these data: that is, we can say that one piece is higher or lower, greater or lesser, than another is. However, ordinal data do not have specific values, so we cannot measure an exact value between them. For example, I freely admit that my baseball skills are poor, my husband's are fair, and my sons' are excellent. I can put these in order from worse to better, but I cannot really measure the distance between my skill level and that of my husband, or between his skill level and that of my sons.

**Table 2-2   Examples of ordinal data**

| Variable | Ordinal data |
| --- | --- |
| Condition of the municipal building | Poor, fair, excellent |
| Level of education completed | Grade school, high school, college, postgraduate |
| Satisfaction with municipal service | Unsatisfied, neutral, satisfied |
| Heat in salsa | Mild, medium, hot, inferno |
| Critic's opinion of movies | One star, two stars, three stars |

In the last example, you might argue that a movie with two stars is twice as good as a movie with one star, but most movie critics would not be that precise. In fact, that is a good way to describe ordinal data. They give you a sense of the order of items, but they are not precise.

> Data are the building blocks of any research,
> and good data are those that are both valid and reliable.

### Interval data

The last type of data, and the type you are probably most familiar with, is interval data, as shown in Table 2–3. **Interval data** are numerical, with equal intervals between values. Interval data are found everywhere in research. In fact, many researchers are uncomfortable working with anything other than interval data. Perhaps, because it is often necessary to count and code nominal and ordinal data into numbers for computers to "read," all data might ultimately be considered interval in natural. However, that is a false conclusion. As mentioned, dummy variables are coded 1 or 0 just to represent two different categories, such as employed or unemployed. Interval data alone are precise. The distance between 12 and 13, and 23 and 24, and 12,852 and 12,853 is the same. Also, the interval of 1 can be divided into smaller and smaller equal units.

Table 2-3    Examples of interval data from three cities

| Variable | Interval data | | |
| --- | --- | --- | --- |
| | City 1 | City 2 | City 3 |
| Department budget subtotals | $82,000 | $95,000 | $225,000 |
| Vehicles in motor fleet | 24 | 3 | 45 |
| Parking space size | 160 cubic feet | 180 cubic feet | 175 cubic feet |
| New employees in FY 2010 | 16 | 54 | 0 |
| Degrees too cold the thermostat is set in the manager's office | 2 | 5 | 12 |

The key characteristic of interval data is precision. And as we learned in the last chapter, the idea of precision is linked to the statistical concept of *reliability*. But reliable data are not necessarily valid, or what we might think of as accurately capturing a concept. Think about what you see when you step on and off a scale several times. Usually the scale will give you about the same reading, the same number of pounds, each time you step on it. The number of pounds shown each time is interval data. This is a relatively precise measurement.

However, does the number of pounds really represent whether someone is fat, skinny, or just right? Obviously not. It is not necessarily, by itself, a valid measure of health or body image. It is only a valid measurement of weight. How we view ourselves is much more complex and can't be represented by a single number. It is better to use many concepts in combination to measure whether or not someone is "just right." This is why everyone from school nurses to personal trainers refers to *body mass index,* a combination of different physical attributes. So while researchers tend to love interval data because they are easy to use with math and computers, in the big picture interval data are limited. Interval data are not any better or worse than nominal or ordinal data; they are just different. Do not mistake the precise nature of interval data as being a claim to the most accurate way to measure a concept.

> The best analyses combine all three types of information:
> nominal, ordinal, and interval.

### Labeling types of data

Why do we worry so much about labeling the type of data we are going to use? In the coming chapters you will see that how we want to measure a concept will determine the statistical methods we use, and in turn, the actual data we collect. Data are the building blocks of any research, and good data are those that are both valid and reliable. Nominal and ordinal data can be less than precise, or vague, but they can also better capture a concept. However, because they are not precise, it is much harder to use statistics with them. Interval data are a mathematically inclined scientist's dream, but they can be limited by their precision: they measure a concept in only one defined way. This book talks about statistical methods to use with different kinds of data, but in the big picture, the best analyses combine all three types of information.

### Levels of data

When looking at data, you need to know not only what kind they are but also from what level. What does that mean? If you think about it, the phrase "looking at data" is very appropriate here. In the same way that we might zoom in close with a camera to capture a person's face, or zoom out to capture a whole class, or really zoom out to take a picture of a whole school, we need to understand if our information is from a person, a school, a municipality, a county, a state, or a country. The level of information is called the **unit of analysis.**

When you have gathered information on a number of units (people, schools, departments, cities, etc.), you have a *data series* (which we'll discuss later in this chapter).

The last two examples in Table 2–4 are interesting. It is probably obvious that if you have a list of numbers from different parking spaces, the unit of analysis is parking space. However, the next example is not so clear. If you have a list of average parking space sizes, the unit of analysis is the area from which the average parking

Table 2-4    Examples of data series and units of analysis

| Data series | Unit of analysis |
| --- | --- |
| Salaries of Tom, Dick, and Harry | Individual or person |
| Weight of Peter, Paul, and Mary | Individual or person |
| Number of employees for each state | State |
| Size of municipal parking spaces | Parking space |
| Average size of parking spaces | Neighborhood, municipality, county, or state |

space size comes. That is, you might have to be specific about whether the average is of all spaces in a neighborhood, a municipality, or a county. The average will have been calculated from individual observations from someone measuring different parking spaces (a fun summer job for an MPA intern, I think), but the average is calculated across the entire unit of analysis and is recorded as the average parking space size for that unit of analysis. For example, if municipalities are the unit of analysis, there is only one average parking space size for all of Council Top. Thus, Council Top is one observation for this unit of analysis.

### Variables

When you collect data, you are collecting information on a **variable.** A variable is just a fancy word for a characteristic that varies from observation to observation regardless of whether the data are nominal, ordinal, or interval. For example, height or political opinion varies across people, and religious nature of government or gross national product varies across countries.

It may seem obvious, but to do any kind of statistical analysis, you need to have information on variables. This means that the data on a characteristic must vary across observations. But sometimes we forget this simple lesson. If all Girl Scouts are girls, it doesn't make much sense in a study on Girl Scouts to have a variable on sex to determine whether the Girl Scout is a boy or a girl. To take a lesson from my son's homework, you might ask if some kinds of turtles are reptiles and some are not. But all turtles are reptiles! The reptile "status" of turtles doesn't change or vary. In other words, it is not a variable.

### The data on a characteristic must vary across observations.

It is sometimes easy to fall into the trap of gathering information on a variable that doesn't really vary. In research I was completing on why people visit nonprofit food pantries, I gathered information on whether the individuals had to apply for food stamps. At the first pantry I visited, I duly started to record this information. It was included in the files for the clients. Halfway through the day I realized that the records showed every person as receiving or having applied for food stamps.

An inquiry to the pantry director cleared up the situation. Clients only received assistance from the pantry if they were already on or had applied for food stamps; so everyone was! I had wasted time and effort recording information that did not vary. I tried to ease my embarrassment by noting that the client files were also including information that was not necessary, so I was not alone. Then the pantry director told me that the staff used the records for federal reporting requirements as part of a grant application, and while it didn't make sense to him, the staff recorded what the government told them to record in order to get the funding. After rethinking my research, I realized that I did not want to capture whether the person had applied for food stamps but whether he or she was actually receiving food stamps.

This is a good example of how the research process is flexible and fluid. I had the same idea of wanting to know if people were using both government and nonprofit food assistance, but I realized that how I had operationalized this idea originally was incorrect. The data I had been gathering was not really answering my question. It was a research design flaw, and therefore I did not have a valid design. Luckily, I was able to change my question and still use the same data to get the answer; I did not have to throw out the whole study and start from scratch! When I revisited the data, there was variation, and whether clients were or were not receiving food stamps became an important factor in understanding hunger in the end.

Variation makes statistics possible. Conducting research with statistics is possible only because you are looking for change: if it happens, where it happens, and why. Another way to think about it is that we are looking for patterns. This is the guiding reason why more pieces of information are generally better than fewer pieces. You can imagine a television screen with few pixels: the picture is not very clear. The more pixels, the sharper the image, the more able you are to tell one object from another. In the same way, the more observations or data points, the clearer we are able to see, for example, how training programs influence worker productivity, or whether a holiday or a pay increase is the better way to raise employee morale. The more data, the stronger the patterns (if they exist), and the more confident we are in our claims about the presence or absence of these patterns.

Variation makes statistics possible.
We are looking for patterns.

Be sure to note, however, that at the extreme, an abundance of data can include what we'll call "white noise." That is, just like a live music recording can include background sounds such as someone in the audience sneezing or the distant roar of a highway, very large data sets, usually containing thousands and thousands of observations, can include some irrelevant information. In those cases, the job of the researchers is to cheer about how much data they have and then take a deep breath before digging in to **clean the data** (another common but not always fun job for an MPA intern). Just like a music engineer might clean out the sound of sneezing from the recording, the researcher will clean out problem data points (more on recognizing those later in the book when we consider outliers) and organize the information before analyzing it.

Even after we clean out obvious problem data points, there will always be some random variation in the data. Little in nature tends to line up perfectly, and strong connections between two things, such as the local economy and minor crime rates, are not linear. The picture will not be entirely, totally, 20/20 clear. But we try to get as close as possible.

## Kinds of data sets

So far in this chapter, we have talked about understanding the basics of what data are. In addition to the type of data (nominal, ordinal, or interval) and the level of data (unit of analysis), you need to understand what kind of data set you have. When you have gathered a group of observations or several series of pieces of information, or data, you have a **data set.** Data sets consist of those individual **data series:** streams or lists of information, such as the batting record for a baseball player for each of the past twenty years. The individual pieces of information or observations, such as the batting average for that player in a particular year, are the **data points.**

For the remainder of this chapter we will discuss three types of data sets: cross sectional, longitudinal or time series, and panel. Instead of saying, we have a certain kind of data set; we instead use shorthand "stats speak" of sorts and qualify the data by the kind of data set, simply saying we have cross-sectional data, longitudinal data, and so on.

## Cross-sectional data

**Cross-sectional data** cut across our units of analysis. It is easy to think of this in almost a physical sense. Cross-sectional data cut through, or across, things as they occur at one point in time. You might gather data—for example, students' reading scores—across schools, cities, or states. Each observation represents a different place or person, but all you gather observations or the same point in time and compile them into a list of reading scores. Cross-sectional data are the most common type of data for comparisons, which may be why public administration uses them so much. Managers and elected officials are always interested in how their jurisdiction or department compares to another. If I were interested in testing my guess (or hypothesis) that rural areas have larger parking spaces than urban areas (adding in population just for fun), I would set up a cross-sectional table like Table 2–5, in which the unit of analysis is the municipality and my variables are size of parking spaces, rural or urban, and overall population.

Table 2-5   Example of a cross-sectional data set

| Municipalities | Size of parking spaces | Rural or urban | Overall population |
|---|---|---|---|
| Municipality 1 | | | |
| Municipality 2 | | | |
| Municipality 3 | | | |
| Municipality 4 | | | |
| Municipality 5 | | | |

### Longitudinal or time-series data

**Longitudinal** or **time-series data** cut across time. Time-series and time-trend data are the same. Usually we look at just one or two variables and see how they have changed over time. You might gather data across years, months, weeks, or days to see if you are doing better or worse than at some time in the past. The political question "Are you better off than four years ago?" is exactly that kind of comparison. The pattern of rising and falling gas prices over the years is another example. If I'm considering moving to Iowa, I might want to know if the economy there (in terms of the gross domestic product, or GDP) is more or less stable over time compared to that of North Carolina and of the country as a whole. My time-series table would look like Table 2–6, in which the unit of analysis is the year.

Table 2-6   Example of a time-series data set

| Year | Growth in North Carolina GDP | Growth in Iowa GDP | Growth in national GDP |
|---|---|---|---|
| 2005 | | | |
| 2006 | | | |
| 2007 | | | |
| 2008 | | | |
| 2009 | | | |

In this example, I am looking at the same variable (GDP) over time, in three different locations: North Carolina, Iowa, and the nation. This allows me to look at the trends for that variable in those different locations over time so that I can compare the rise and fall of the economy in those locations over the same period.

I could also look at the same location but at different variables within it, comparing the rise and fall of different things in the same place over time, as in Table 2–7. In this example, my unit of analysis is still the year, but my variables are now based on one location, North Carolina, and are growth in GDP, growth in population, and growth in sales tax revenues.

### Table 2-7   Another example of a time-series data set

| Year | North Carolina | | |
| | Growth in GDP | Growth in population | Growth in sales tax revenues |
| --- | --- | --- | --- |
| 2005 | | | |
| 2006 | | | |
| 2007 | | | |
| 2008 | | | |
| 2009 | | | |

## Panel data

What gets tricky is when I try to include different years, different locations, and different variables in the same table. Consider Table 2–8. Is it useful? Why would it be difficult to do an analysis with this table? It is set up with the unit of analysis being the year, but the variables are a hodge-podge of things and places. This is when a **panel data** set like the one shown in Table 2–9 is the answer. Panel data are cross-sectional data over time. Simply put, panel data sets capture data across both time and location.

In this example, the unit of analysis is year/state so that we have observations on variables for different states in different years. You could also look at state/year if you wanted to, such as in Table 2–10. The computer will read the data in the same way. The computer doesn't care about the labels; it will only look for patterns in the data. The labels are for us so that we can make sure we are gathering the right information to answer the question to solve the problem.

### Table 2-8   An example of a troublesome table

| Year | Growth in North Carolina GDP | Growth in Iowa population | Growth in national sales tax revenues |
| --- | --- | --- | --- |
| 2005 | | | |
| 2006 | | | |
| 2007 | | | |
| 2008 | | | |
| 2009 | | | |

Table 2-9     An example of a panel data set

| Year/ state | Growth in GDP | | Growth in population | | Growth in sales tax revenues | |
|---|---|---|---|---|---|---|
| | NC | Iowa | NC | Iowa | NC | Iowa |
| 2005 | | | | | | |
| 2006 | | | | | | |
| 2007 | | | | | | |
| 2008 | | | | | | |
| 2009 | | | | | | |

Table 2-10     Another example of a panel data set

| State/year | Growth in GDP | | | | | Growth in population | | | | | Growth in sales tax revenues | | | | |
|---|---|---|---|---|---|---|---|---|---|---|---|---|---|---|---|
| | 2005 | 2006 | 2007 | 2008 | 2009 | 2005 | 2006 | 2007 | 2008 | 2009 | 2005 | 2006 | 2007 | 2008 | 2009 |
| North Carolina | | | | | | | | | | | | | | | |
| Iowa | | | | | | | | | | | | | | | |

When designing your data set, keep in mind that cross-sectional data are no better or worse than time-series data; they are just different. Whether to gather cross-sectional data or time-series data will depend on what question you are asking. The two types of data sets answer different kinds of questions. Cross-sectional data answer the question of how we compare to others. Time-series data answer the question of how we compare to ourselves over time. Finally, we combine the two: panel data answers the question of how we compare to others over time. Panel data are the richest kind of data because they can look at the issue in both ways.

**Chuck took a quick glance at his reflection** in the windows looking over the parking lot. He wasn't particularly self-conscious, but ever since the meetings started appearing on public access television, he had at least tried to not embarrass himself. Did his wide tie make him look fat? He tried to refocus. *Let's see,* he thought. *What information about inspections could be surprising?*

He turned to Nina. "So, what is surprising? That our average number of home inspections is not very high compared to Neola's?" asked Chuck, looking down at the agenda and referring to the bustling town about twenty-three miles south to which Council Top was always being compared. One of the council members wanted to know why dilapidated homes on the northeast side were not being forced to clean up, and the issue was on the agenda. That was the only thing he could think of. The inspection staff always reported that it led the county in average number of inspections, but Chuck didn't ever see the official numbers.

"That the average number of inspections is not the right number to look at," she replied with a smile.

## Review questions

1. What is the difference between observations and data?
2. What type of data is *ethnicity*? What makes it that type of data?
3. What is an example of ordinal data? What makes it ordinal data?
4. Define the term *variable*.
5. Give an example of a variable and the data to examine within that variable. Example: Sex (variable): female, male (data)
6. What type of variable is each of the following?
   a. Tax I.D. number
   b. Weight
   c. Number of parking spaces
   d. Satisfaction level
   e. Nationality
   f. Employment status
7. Define and give an example of cross-sectional data.
8. What is the difference between *unit of analysis* and *data series*? Give examples of each.
9. Find an example of panel data. How are they organized?

# Bring Some Order to This Chaos!

## 3

## [MORE DESCRIPTIVE STATISTICS]

**Nina approached the microphone** at the front of the room and stood next to Chuck. This was her first time addressing the council, and while outwardly she appeared calm, inside she was nervous. She tried to reassure herself that she was well prepared. She herself had typed every one of these numbers into her spreadsheet, and she knew it better than anyone else did in the room.

Chuck started. "Item 5 on our agenda is the home inspections data review. Last week, in our open comment time, a citizen raised her concerns about the poor condition of houses in the most southern part of Ginger Street. She suggested that the city was not keeping up with home inspections the way it should, comparing us to Neola, which she felt had a good record of home inspections. Council asked my office to explore the issue. In response, Nina Schorn, our new analyst, has prepared a short briefing on the home inspections data. Nina?" said Chuck.

"Thank you, Mr. Edwards. Let me first tell you a little about how we gather the inspections data, and then I'll review some basic descriptive information. Every week, our inspectors conduct dozens of inspections. The department is experimenting with an electronic system in which inspectors will have laptops with them and will record the inspection information directly into their laptops. They will download the information twice a day into a central department database. This will allow for much easier and quicker recording, tracking, and analysis of the data. Unfortunately, the system has a number of bugs in it, and the only person who knows how to run the preset reports on it is on extended disability leave." The eyes of a couple of council members rolled. The portly woman on the end of the council table stifled a laugh. The chair, Leo Berner, was smiling. Leo always smiled.

Nina took a deep breath and continued. "However, I took the past year's data from the paper records on file and entered them into a spreadsheet. And there are some interesting findings when we compare ourselves to Neola."

"I'm almost afraid to ask," interrupted the portly woman. "But how are we doing on average compared to those rapscallions?"

"Last year," said Nina, "we reported that in a typical week, twenty-four inspections were done, compared to an average of forty-three in Neola, but . . . "

"Did you say twenty-four compared to forty-three? That's shameful! What's wrong with our inspection program?" The woman demanded, turning to Chuck.

"I'll speak to the department head this week and ask for an explanation," said Chuck, turning to look at the department head, who was shaking his head. "I'll report back to you personally this week," he hurried to say.

"You don't need to," said Nina loudly. When the room got quiet, she went on. "You don't need to; I can explain it easily. You see, twenty-four is the wrong number to use here. That's the mode. We need to look at the median." The department head looked very relieved.

"What is the mode? Or the median for that matter? I just want what is typical. How about the average?" Leo said.

"In this case, that would be close," she replied, "but it's still not the best way to think of a typical week for our inspections department." Nina clicked on her PowerPoint and started to explain.

S tatistics have two uses: (1) to describe a thing or phenomenon and (2) to infer something about that thing or phenomenon. So it is not a surprise that there are two types of statistics: **descriptive** and **inferential**. This chapter deals with the first part, descriptive statistics.

If something looks odd, it probably is odd.

## Descriptive statistics

Descriptive statistics are the basis, the foundation, for *everything else* in any kind of analysis. If we don't have descriptive statistics, we cannot do any other type of analysis. Yet we often give descriptive statistics short shrift. Averages don't sound exciting unless, perhaps, we're talking baseball; fashion mode is a better conversation starter than numerical mode. Students and well-meaning professionals often attempt to impress others by whipping up a multivariate regression (something you, too, will be able to do by the time you get to the end of this book). However, rushing into something complicated without understanding the basics is a recipe for disaster.

One time I made brownies at my brother's house. My mom, my other brother, and I were visiting him for the weekend. Tired from the long drive, we rented a movie and settled in for the evening. I had a strong desire for something sweet. My brother, living the spartan life of a law student at the time, had a box mix for brownies. He had bought that recently but, unfortunately, not the vegetable oil at the back of the shelf. The immediate lesson I learned that night is that brownies made with rancid oil do not taste *good*.

The larger lesson was that if you do not pay attention to all the ingredients of a recipe, the result can stink. Same with statistics. You need to make sure that all the ingredients—or, in this case, the data—are *good* before combining them. Otherwise, one bad addition can throw off the whole batch. In a kitchen, if you get a whiff of something that smells bad, it probably is bad. In statistics, if something looks odd, it probably is odd. In both cases, you need to examine everything to see what is actually going on.

## Counts and frequency distributions

Let's return to Nina's problem. The council had asked her to examine the data on house inspections. Table 3–1 shows the data she obtained, by week for one year.

**Table 3-1   Housing inspections data for Council Top, January–December 20xx**

| Week in the year | No. of inspections | Week in the year | No. of inspections | Week in the year | No. of inspections | Week in the year | No. of inspections |
|---|---|---|---|---|---|---|---|
| 1 | 12 | 14 | 23 | 27 | 52 | 40 | 48 |
| 2 | 21 | 15 | 100 | 28 | 67 | 41 | 37 |
| 3 | 19 | 16 | 52 | 29 | 89 | 42 | 36 |
| 4 | 29 | 17 | 41 | 30 | 74 | 43 | 34 |
| 5 | 29 | 18 | 78 | 31 | 83 | 44 | 32 |
| 6 | 27 | 19 | 45 | 32 | 99 | 45 | 62 |
| 7 | 49 | 20 | 28 | 33 | 84 | 46 | 35 |
| 8 | 66 | 21 | 0 | 34 | 75 | 47 | 13 |
| 9 | 80 | 22 | 37 | 35 | 74 | 48 | 15 |
| 10 | 64 | 23 | 75 | 36 | 81 | 49 | 29 |
| 11 | 66 | 24 | 89 | 37 | 73 | 50 | 12 |
| 12 | 37 | 25 | 79 | 38 | 91 | 51 | 5 |
| 13 | 68 | 26 | 80 | 39 | 83 | 52 | 0 |

The absolute first step in any kind of data analysis is to look at the information. In our example of house inspections, we are dealing with counts: counting the number of inspections every day, or week, or month. *Counts* refer to data that represent counting the number of times something occurs, such as the number of inspections, or the number of people visiting the tax assessor's office, or the number of structure fires, or the number of false calls. Statisticians also refer to counts as *frequencies*: How frequently are there structural fires in a month? How frequently do citizens visit the assessor's office? Counts, or frequencies, by their nature, are interval data. With interval data, when we just look at all the numbers, it is hard to get a clear picture of the information as a whole. As the famous phrase says, a picture is worth a thousand words, er . . . data points. Our next step may be literally to make a picture: a graph. Figure 3–1 is a simple Excel graph of the number of inspections over the year.

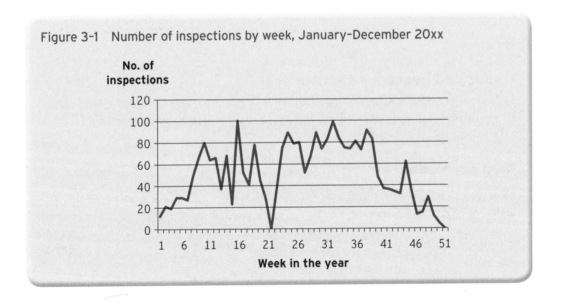

Figure 3-1   Number of inspections by week, January-December 20xx

The information is still hard to read, but let's consider what stands out in the picture. At the beginning of the year, inspections start out slowly; they then increase in the middle of the year before dropping off again. If home inspections follow home construction patterns, the drop-off makes sense. When the weather is better in Council Top, more home construction takes place. Yet something is strange: the observations around week 21 take a nosedive. And as we said, if something looks odd, it probably is odd. In this case, we would call the observation an **outlier:** that is, it lies outside of the normal pattern of the data for the rest of the year.

If I had these data, I would want to know why they took such a steep drop in the 20th and 21st weeks before rebounding in week 22. I can find this out only by actually going back to the original data and asking questions. Did something unusual happen in those weeks? Luckily, when Nina looked into the actual data, she found her answer. The department data were correct. There are two inspectors in the department. In weeks 20 and 21, one of the inspectors took his annual vacation. In weeks 21 and 22, the other inspector took her vacation. This left the department half staffed for the first week, closed for the middle week when both inspectors were on vacation, and half staffed again for the third week. Therefore, during those three weeks, this small department was not operating normally.

## Outliers

Since outliers lie outside of the normal pattern of the data, how will they affect the analysis, and what should you do with them? There are three options for dealing with outliers.

First, if there is an obvious typo or entry mistake, you can correct the data point or points and note the correction. Sometimes those types of mistakes are obvious and allow you to legitimately correct the data. This is part of cleaning the data, as I mentioned in Chapter 2. But if you cannot confirm it is a mistake, you must assume that the data are correct and that something else is coming into play (such as the department staff vacation schedules).

Second, you can keep all observations in the data set, including the outliers, so that they have as much **weight,** or impact, as any other piece of data. This would be the position of data purists, who decline to change any aspect of a data set for fear of introducing bias. The benefit of keeping the outlier in is that no one can accuse you of manipulating the data set. Also, unless you know why there is an outlier (such as department staff vacation schedules), you do not have a legitimate basis for throwing it out. If the department was fully staffed and we could not identify anything else going on, we would note that it was an outlier but probably keep it in our analysis. The "cost" of keeping the data point in is that it is so different from all the other data points. It creates a skew, or extension, in the data in a way that if you only look at a single descriptive number like the average, you don't realize that with the outlier in, the average is very different from what it would be with the outlier excluded. The outlier has a large impact on how we think about the data. It extends our data a lot, in a high or low direction. (More about skew later in this chapter.) This can become a real problem with extreme outliers.

Third, you can exclude, or throw out, the outlier, arguing that it is not representative of the true pattern of the data. In this case, the benefit is that the "normal" pattern becomes clearer. The cost is that we, as analysts, have used our subjective judgment to throw the data point out, and therefore we can be accused of manipulating the results. For example, a data purist would argue that the outlier is just as "normal" as all the other data points. This is a legitimate argument. With housing inspections, if employees take vacation at the same point each year, year in and year out, the normal pattern is one that includes a large drop-off in inspections during that particular time.

As a practitioner, I recommend that you not try to be a data purist. If you are able to determine *why* an outlier is an outlier, but you don't think that it represents the true nature of what you are examining, then consider excluding it from the data set. A guiding question you can ask yourself is whether including the outlier in your analysis increases or decreases the validity and reliability of the data set based on what you know about the outlier, your data set, and the nature of your research. Remember: the big picture question at hand is whether the data are good—not perfect! If you believe that throwing out an outlier more accurately and precisely represents the "normal" or true pattern of the data, then throw it out (but be prepared to justify why you did so).

If you are still not sure whether throwing out an outlier would be legitimate, then settle the issue quickly by taking both approaches! Show your information and analysis both with and without the outliers, and let the audience be the judge. Either way, organize and LOOK at all of your data. Do not rely on summary statistics. Figure 3–2 shows the same information but without the three outliers previously identified.

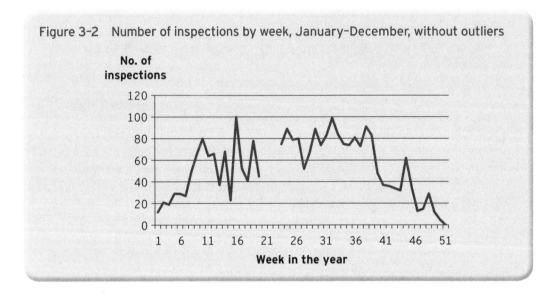

Figure 3-2    Number of inspections by week, January–December, without outliers

**No. of inspections**

**Week in the year**

### Smoothing data

Looking back at our data in Table 3–1, we can see how the pictures we drew in Figures 3–1 and 3–2 are beginning to help us look clearly at the information in the data. We can even take this process one step further by **smoothing the data** so that the graph shows the general patterns without all the individual spikes and valleys. To do this, we simply add a trend line through the data, as shown in Figure 3–3. The trend line is made by creating a new data series of **moving averages**—in this case, where each point is the average of five years of values: the point in the middle, plus the two years before and the two years after. Luckily, most spreadsheet software packages can add trend lines with a keystroke, and you can customize your trend line to be straight or curved, a moving average of any number of years, or any other type of line. The more years you use to create the moving average, the smoother the data line becomes.

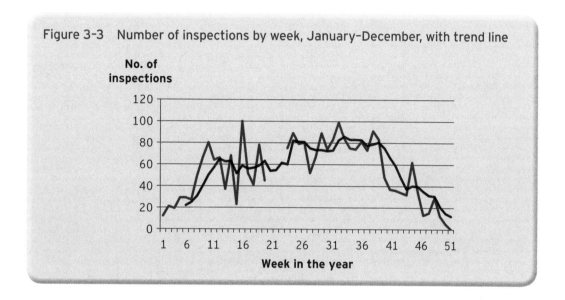

Figure 3-3   Number of inspections by week, January–December, with trend line

We already had a picture that communicates in detail how inspection workload increases and decreases through the year. The only value of smoothed data is that if the original data jumps around a lot, smoothed data may make the general pattern easier to see and follow. The small, individual deviations from the overall pattern are less of a distraction.

## Data distribution

This is only the start, though. We have a sense of how the data change over time, but not if they are high or low compared to other municipalities or to ourselves in other years. To get that kind of picture, we need to organize the information so that it creates a snapshot, just as a television organizes each pixel in such a way that when we step back far enough, we see an image. We need to know the **data distribution**, and we start by organizing the data from small to large, or vice versa. If we reorganize the data from small to large, our table would read like Table 3–2.

***Frequency distribution***   As you can tell, a really long, continuous column of numbers isn't very helpful for making decisions, either. This is the value of descriptive

Table 3-2    Home inspections by week, from lowest number of inspections to highest

| Week in the year | No. of inspections | Week in the year | No. of inspections | Week in the year | No. of inspections | Week in the year | No. of inspections |
|---|---|---|---|---|---|---|---|
| 21 | 0 | 5 | 29 | 16 | 52 | 18 | 78 |
| 52 | 0 | 49 | 29 | 27 | 52 | 25 | 79 |
| 51 | 5 | 44 | 32 | 45 | 62 | 9 | 80 |
| 1 | 12 | 43 | 34 | 10 | 64 | 26 | 80 |
| 50 | 12 | 46 | 35 | 8 | 66 | 36 | 81 |
| 47 | 13 | 42 | 36 | 11 | 66 | 31 | 83 |
| 48 | 15 | 12 | 37 | 28 | 67 | 39 | 83 |
| 3 | 19 | 22 | 37 | 13 | 68 | 33 | 84 |
| 2 | 21 | 41 | 37 | 37 | 73 | 24 | 89 |
| 14 | 23 | 17 | 41 | 30 | 74 | 29 | 89 |
| 6 | 27 | 19 | 45 | 35 | 74 | 38 | 91 |
| 20 | 28 | 40 | 48 | 23 | 75 | 32 | 99 |
| 4 | 29 | 7 | 49 | 34 | 75 | 15 | 100 |

statistics. Descriptive statistics provide us with shortcuts to understand where the data are concentrated or clustered and how they are distributed. One of the first ways to get a handle on lots of data is to group them. For example, instead of listing the number 37 three times in Table 3-2 for the number of inspections by week, we can shorten the list by listing each number and then how often that particular number occurs, or the **frequency** of that particular number. For example, we would show the number 37 and that it occurred 3 times. With that, our table might look like Table 3-3.

We have now moved from a graduated list of the number of weekly inspections to a **frequency distribution.** In this case, the frequency distribution is not much of an improvement over the really long column in Table 3-2; the difference between some of these numbers (say, 89 and 91 inspections) is not that great. We could easily further collapse the data into groups or bins to produce Table 3-4. This example collapses the data for the number of inspections into bins of "tens."

***Percentage distribution.***    You'll see that in addition to the frequency distribution, I included a **percentage distribution**. For each bin of tens, I calculated the percentage of weeks out of the total that fell into that group. For example, there were three weeks in which the number of inspections was between 0 and 10. These three weeks, divided by the total number of weeks (52), equals 5.7%. In this way, we are able to determine where the bulk of our observations fall. Table 3-4 tells us that Council Top's inspection department did between 51 and 60 inspections a week in 2 separate weeks, or nearly 4%

## Table 3-3   Frequency distribution of home inspections

| No. of inspections | Frequency distribution (no. of weeks) | No. of inspections | Frequency distribution (no. of weeks) | No. of inspections | Frequency distribution (no. of weeks) | No. of inspections | Frequency distribution (no. of weeks) |
|---|---|---|---|---|---|---|---|
| 0 | 2 | 29 | 3 | 52 | 2 | 79 | 1 |
| 5 | 1 | 32 | 1 | 62 | 1 | 80 | 2 |
| 12 | 2 | 34 | 1 | 64 | 1 | 81 | 1 |
| 13 | 1 | 35 | 1 | 66 | 2 | 83 | 2 |
| 15 | 1 | 36 | 1 | 67 | 1 | 84 | 1 |
| 19 | 1 | 37 | 3 | 68 | 1 | 89 | 2 |
| 21 | 1 | 41 | 1 | 73 | 1 | 91 | 1 |
| 23 | 1 | 45 | 1 | 74 | 2 | 99 | 1 |
| 27 | 1 | 48 | 1 | 75 | 2 | 100 | 1 |
| 28 | 1 | 49 | 1 | 78 | 1 | | |

of the year; however, it did between 31 and 40 inspections a week in 7 separate weeks, or 13.5% of the year.

A percentage distribution table allows us to be even more specific: we can determine where the bottom 25% and top 25% of observations fall. We can tell what point is in the exact middle: the point at which 50% of the weeks (26) had a lower number of inspections and 50% of the weeks had a higher number of inspections. In this case, it

## Table 3-4   Frequency distribution table

| No. of inspections | Frequency distribution (no. of weeks) | Percentage distribution (% of total weeks) |
|---|---|---|
| 0–10 | 3 | 5.7 |
| 11–20 | 5 | 9.6 |
| 21–30 | 7 | 13.5 |
| 31–40 | 7 | 13.5 |
| 41–50 | 4 | 7.7 |
| 51–60 | 2 | 3.9 |
| 61–70 | 6 | 11.5 |
| 71–80 | 7 | 13.5 |
| 81–90 | 8 | 15.4 |
| 91–100 | 3 | 5.7 |

is between 41 and 50, and 51 and 60. One-half of the weeks had 50 or fewer inspections, and one-half had 51 or more. The major break points, which are at 25%, 50%, and 75%, are called **quartiles,** meaning that each represents a quarter of all the data points. From the top of the lower quartile to the bottom of the upper quartile (from 25% of observations to 75% of observations) is called the **interquartile**

**range** since it represents the inner portion, or middle section of observations.

Frequency distributions are great tools to use because you can also take any particular value and find out what percentage of observations lies above that number and what percentage lies below it. Table 3–5, for example, is the same as Table 3–4, but now it includes a cumulative frequency distribution and cumulative percentage distribution.

Table 3-5    Frequency, cumulative frequency, percentage, and cumulative percentage distributions

| No. of inspections | Frequency distribution (no. of weeks) | Cumulative frequency distribution | Percentage distribution (% of total weeks) | Cumulative percentage distribution |
|---|---|---|---|---|
| 0–10 | 3 | 3 | 5.7 | 5.7 |
| 11–20 | 5 | 8 | 9.6 | 15.3 |
| 21–30 | 7 | 15 | 13.5 | 28.8 |
| 31–40 | 7 | 22 | 13.5 | 42.3 |
| 41–50 | 4 | 26 | 7.7 | 50.0 |
| 51–60 | 2 | 28 | 3.9 | 53.9 |
| 61–70 | 6 | 34 | 11.5 | 65.4 |
| 71–80 | 7 | 41 | 13.5 | 78.9 |
| 81–90 | 8 | 49 | 15.4 | 94.3 |
| 91–100 | 3 | 52 | 5.7 | 100.0 |

Remember how in Figure 3–3 we saw our data visually with a trendline chart? We can also see data visually with a histogram, as shown in Figure 3–4. In a histogram, we create a number of "bins" for our data, such as 0–10 inspections, 11–20 inspections, 21–30 inspections, etc. The number of weeks that fit into that bin is the frequency for that particular bin. A histogram of frequencies then allows us to see quickly how many weeks fit into the 0–10 inspection bin, the 11–20 inspection bin, etc. If Nina presented this chart to the council, she would be able to communicate a lot of information in a single figure. A simple look suggests that the data are in two main groups, a higher group and a lower group.

To go a step further, you can add in the cumulative percentages, as shown in Figure 3–5. The line represents how each group adds to the total percentage. A place where the line is steep represents that the number of weeks in that range is a lot relative to the total number of weeks. A place where the line is flat means that the number of weeks in that range is small relative to the total. However, I do not recommend using this kind of graph with too many audiences; it can get too confusing too quickly. If Nina presented this chart to the council, she would likely get many blank looks until she walked members through it. The lesson to remember is that sometimes, less information is better. Communicate just what you need to communicate to make your point.

Even with all these data, we still may be left with the question of what is the number of inspections in a typical week! That question takes us to the next section: measures of central tendency.

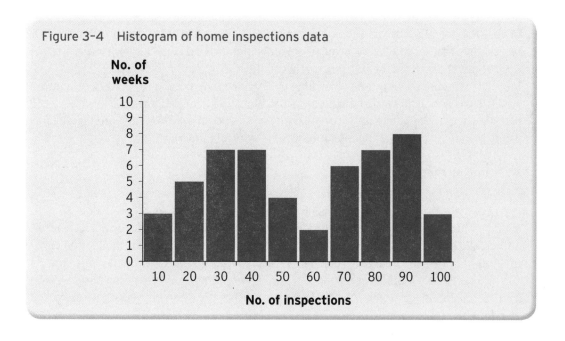

Figure 3-4 Histogram of home inspections data

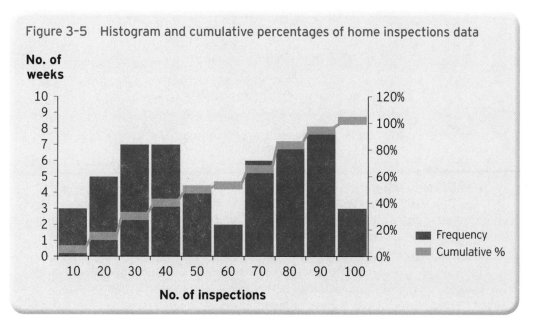

Figure 3-5 Histogram and cumulative percentages of home inspections data

## Measures of central tendency: Mean, median, and mode

People generally want to know what is typical. What is a typical day like? What does a typical citizen look like? What would I expect to find in a typical house? In statistics, we capture the idea of "typical" by calculating different values, but first, we need to put bookends around our data; in statistical terms, we first identify the **range** of our data. In this case, the range of values goes from a couple of weeks in which the number of inspections was 10 or under to a couple of weeks in which the number was close to 100. Specifically, the range is the difference between the lowest and highest values. With a low of 0 inspections in one week and a high of 100 in another, the range for our example is 100. This gives us the top and bottom, but we are still looking for the typical value. Statistically speaking, there are three different ways to be "typical." We refer to the three values *mean*, *median*, and *mode* as **measures of central tendency**.

### Average, or mean

First, we look for the **average,** or, in statistical terms, the **mean.** The terms *mean* and *average* is the same thing. To calculate the mean, you add up all the values in a data series and divide by the total number of values. In our running example, you add up all the numbers of inspections from all the weeks (2677), and then divide by the number of weeks in a year (52). The result is 51.48. If you round that value (it is silly to report a fraction of an inspection), the mean number of inspections in a week for Council Top is 52. If you want to impress your friends at lunch, you could casually draw the formula for the mean on a napkin:

$$\mu = (\Sigma X)/N,$$

where $\mu$ is the Greek letter mu, the notation for "mean"

$\Sigma$ is the notation for "sum of"

$X$ is the notation for a variable—usually, a series of numbers ($X_1$, $X_2$, $X_3$, . . . or if you were measuring length of something like a vacation, 23 days, 6 days, 13 days, . . .)

$N$ is the number of numbers (such as having data about 45 different employee vacations).

The average is probably the most widely used descriptive statistic and also probably the most misused. Averages work really well when data are normally distributed. We'll discuss normal distribution much more in the coming chapters, but for right now, imagine a normal curve as a bell-shaped curve such as the one in Figure 3–6, where most values are in the middle, some are at the high end, and some are at the low end.

The thing to remember about averages is that they can change dramatically based on a single number or a few numbers in the series—the outliers—that are very high or very low relative to the rest of the numbers. Average income in the state of

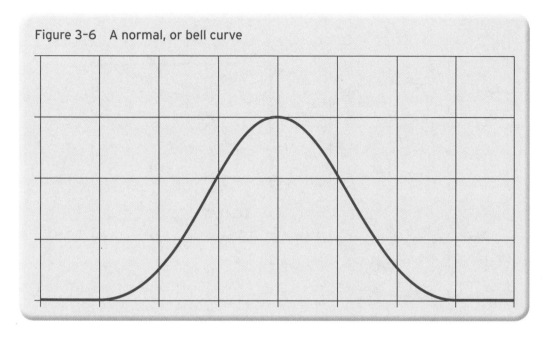

Figure 3-6   A normal, or bell curve

Washington, for example, may not be a good measure of the income of a typical person in a random Washington town. Why? Well, Bill Gates, the multibillionaire of Microsoft computer fame, lives there. His income would shift the average from what we consider typical to a higher number. The same is the case with Warren Buffett, Bill's multibillionaire friend in Omaha, Nebraska. Average income in Omaha would be much higher if Buffett's income were included in the calculation. In our running example of home inspections, the weeks when the number of inspections was zero because the inspectors were on vacation are clearly not typical inspection weeks. Those outlier values of zero pull the average down lower than what we would expect for a typical week. When we have these types of extreme values, we say the data are **skewed.**

## Bill Gates's income can really "skew" things up.

When statisticians hear that data are skewed, they automatically know it really means the data are "screwed up by outliers." What they are then interested in knowing is *how* the data are skewed: is the outlier on the high end or on the low end? If it is on the low end, the curve stretches out to the left, in a negative direction, to include the outlier. In this case, as shown in Figure 3–7, the data distribution has a **negative skew.** If the outliers are on the high end, the curve stretches out to the right, or in a positive direction, in which case the data distribution has a **positive skew.** Including Bill Gates's income would give our data a positive skew.

Figure 3-7   Skewed data

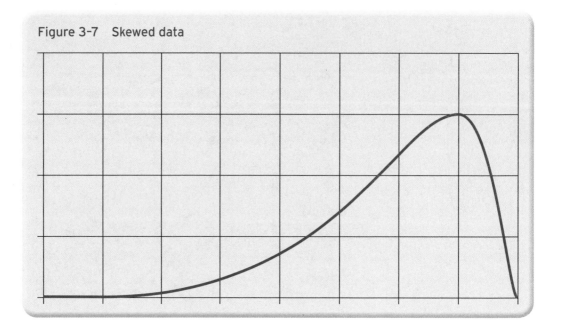

## Median

If we cannot use the average, then, how else can we measure what would be the typical value of a data series? An alternative would be the **median**—literally, the middle value. The median is the value above which and below which 50% of the data series falls. If your data series were 1, 2, 3, 4, and 5, the median would be the number 3 because half of the other numbers (numbers 1 and 2) fall below it and the other half (numbers 4 and 5) fall above it.

The median is easy to identify in a data set that comprises an odd number of observations, or data points, because there is a middle number. If there is an even number of data points, however, there is not a value that falls in the exact middle. In that case, the median is halfway between the middle two values. Thus, if our data series were 1, 2, 3, 4, 5, and 6, the median would be 3.5 or the average of the middle two values.

In our inspections data, we have 52 observations: the number of housing inspections each week for 52 weeks, one calendar year. If we put the data in order of lowest to highest value, that is, the lowest number of housing inspections in a week to the highest number of housing inspections in a week, and then split the data into two groups, we would have 26 weeks in the lower half and 26 weeks in the higher half.

Look at Table 3–2. There is not one middle observation; 52 is an even number. Because there is not a middle observation, the median would the number of housing inspections halfway between the number of inspections in the 26th and 27th observations. The 26th observation is the number of inspections for the 7th week: 49 inspections. The 27th observation is the number of inspections for the 16th week:

52 inspections. The exact middle between 49 inspections and 52 inspections is 50.5 (for the math nerds out there, 52 – 49 = 3. And 3/2 = 1.5. Add 1.5 to the lower of the two starting values, 49: 49 + 1.5 = 50.5). The median for our data set is 50.5. There are 26 observations below this value and 26 observations above. Or, in other words, 50% of the observations are above this value and 50% of the observations are below.

| Table 3-6 | Home inspections, by week, FY 20xx, using individual data |
|---|---|
| Statistic | Value |
| Number of weeks included in analysis | 48 (excludes 4 weeks that are outliers due to employee vacations or holidays) |
| Minimum | 5 |
| Maximum | 100 |
| Range | 95 (5 to 100) |
| Mean | 54 |
| Median | 57 |
| Mode | 29, 37 |

Whenever there are outliers in data, researchers tend to use the median as a typical value rather than the average. Medians are not skewed by outliers. This is why analyses often use median income instead of average income. The same logic applies to median house value or property tax bill or utility bill: in all cases, the average could easily be skewed by extremely low or high values.

> If there are extreme values in your data set,
> use the median instead of the mean.

## Mode

So, is the median the best measure of a typical value? That is, does it best show where the central bulk of the data lie? Not always. Like means, medians can also fool us, although it is less likely. Maybe the **mode** would work? The mode represents the most common single value—in other words, the value that occurs most frequently. In our data set, if we look down the list, there were three weeks when 29 inspections were completed. There were also 3 weeks when 37 inspections were completed. These are both modes, the most frequently occurring number of inspections in a week. So, is 29 or 37 the typical number of housing inspections? Well, there are an awful lot of weeks where there were more inspections. So, what do we do?

Maybe the solution is to use not the detailed data but the data as they are grouped for the histogram in Figure 3–4. When we look at that image, we get a better sense of the "big picture." Unfortunately, our data represent a **bimodal distribution,** more like two normal curves next to each other. There are two main clusters of data instead of one; there is a cluster of data around 20–40 inspections and a cluster of data around 70–90 inspections. But this fits with the big picture; in general, there are lower numbers of inspections in the parts of the year when the weather is poor and higher numbers in the parts of the year when the weather is better.

Another example of a bimodal distribution could be a political position on a controversial issue, such as immigration. A large group of people is favorable toward increasing immigration, while another large group of people is not favorable toward increasing immigration. People tend to be at one end or another. But there are many fewer people who fall directly in the middle, with no preference in one direction or the other.

## Mean, median, and mode together

So, like the average, there are times when the median is not the best to use. And, as with our bimodal distribution, there are times when the mode is not good either. The average, median, and mode all have strengths and weaknesses when used as the sole piece of information to show what a typical value is or on central tendency. If the mean is higher than the median, you know that there is an outlier with a high value skewing the curve in a positive direction. If the mean is lower than the median, you know that there is an outlier with a low value skewing the curve in a negative direction. If the mode is different from the mean and median, again, there is some skew to the data. But put the mean, the median, and the mode together, and they can be very powerful. Together, they can tell you a lot about the distribution of your data. For example, in one instance where the value of the mean, the median, and the mode is the same occurs in a normal curve!

When in doubt, show the picture.
Then you don't need to say much else.

- The power of simply taking the raw data and organizing it is clear. We can easily get a visual of the distribution of that data by using a simple line graph, histogram, or other type of graph or chart. With the data and graphs of the number of home inspections by week that we have used in this chapter, we can provide our elected officials with the following information for home inspections in Council Top:

- The number of inspections varied a great deal, between 0 and 100 inspections per week. Generally, the department was able to conduct from about 30 to 80 inspections per week. The median number of inspections was around 50.

- The data revealed two weeks when no inspections were done, but these were Christmas week and a week in the spring when both inspectors were on vacation. In two other weeks, only one inspector was on duty. In parts of our analysis, we did not include these "outliers."

- The number of inspections seems to follow patterns for housing construction, as you might expect; lower in the winter but peaking in the middle-to-late summer/early fall.

You will notice that I used the terms *about* and *around*. That is not because I don't know the exact numbers; in fact it is easy, with a touch of a button in spreadsheet software programs, to find out the basic descriptive statistics down to multiple decimal points. But don't be dazzled by data. Precision to the *n*th degree is generally not the hallmark of good statistical communicators. It is especially silly to use decimals when speaking of things that can't be divided, such as people. Nobel Prize–winning economists are often those who can put complex behavior into simple, easily understood terms.

## Nina finished up, having been concise, concrete, and free of ambiguity, just as she had learned in her public administration program.

"So we used the wrong number last year?" Council Member Whitaker didn't sound too surprised.

"I never did understand where that number came from. It seemed far too low to us," the department manager said.

"Well, for some reason, I feel we won't have the same problem this year," Chuck said, looking at Nina with a slight smile.

### Review questions

1. Why are the statistics in this chapter called "descriptive"?
2. What would be a reason to use descriptive statistics? Give examples of possible uses.
3. What is an outlier, and how can it affect data?
4. Give the three ways to deal with an outlier in a data set. What would be the effect of each?
5. What would a data purist do with an outlier, and why?
6. When would it be appropriate to use a moving average?
7. From what you've seen in the various tables and charts in this chapter, if you were to hire a part-time temporary employee to help with home inspections, during what time of year would you hire someone? For how many months? Justify your answer.
8. Would you show your council figures that show each data point, or figures that show grouped data? Why?
9. Describe each of the measures of central tendency and how it is calculated:
   a. Mean
   b. Median
   c. Mode
10. In a data set, if the mean is lower than the median, what can we say about the data?

# The Picture Is Becoming Clearer

## 4

## [YET *MORE* DESCRIPTIVE STATISTICS]

**Chuck saw the light on in Nina's office** when he was walking out Thursday night. "How come you're staying late?"

"Remember the presentation of the inspections data last month?"

"Yeah, you were the talk of the council! At least until Wednesday, when the sewer backed up in the city jail."

"Well, after that, the budget director asked me to do some research on debt at both the state and local levels. We might need to issue bonds for new wastewater treatment and sewer improvements. At first I didn't think it would be a big deal, but it's more complicated than you think." Nina sounded tired, but you couldn't mistake the underlying interest in her voice. "I just have the state data right now. You see, first I had to find out where to get the data—the budget director wants information on general obligation debt—and then I had to understand whether general obligation (GO) debt was defined the same way in each state. You can't mix apples and oranges, you know, or it screws up the entire analysis." Nina wasn't looking at Chuck anymore; she was flipping through her spreadsheets. Her words picked up speed, and Chuck knew she was "in the zone"—what he called it when she was focused and excited about her information.

"I started to come up with a lot of states that didn't have any GO debt at all. Zero. Like Arizona. I thought it was just being very fiscally responsible at first, but actually, Arizona prohibits the use of general obligation debt. So I realized I first had to find out what states are statutorily allowed to carry GO debt and then look at their debt levels."

"That's good, Nina," said Chuck, as he edged toward the door. Nina didn't seem to notice. She went on, "But once you get the right data and the right states and the right organization, you see some great stuff."

"Great. Well, I have to go home to catch the news. . . ."

"But of course, if you just look at total debt levels by state, you realize that some big states have a lot of debt, and some smaller states have a small amount of debt, and it is more than likely just a function of the state size. So I have to control for that by putting the data into per-capita terms."

Chuck couldn't help himself. "What does 'per-capita terms' mean?"

"Per person. And when you do that, you can see how spread out the data are. You get this." Nina swiveled the computer screen so Chuck could see it in the doorway.

"Wow—and where are we?" Chuck stepped back into the room.

In the last chapter we talked about measures of central tendency, primarily the mean, median, and mode. But knowing the center point of your data is like only seeing someone's belly button. You have no idea what the entire person really looks like. We need to see the whole form.

We got the outline of that form through other measures discussed in the last chapter: the range, which tells us the lowest and highest numbers, and the quartiles, the numbers that sit at the 25th, 50th, and 75th percentile points of the data. The "picture" of the data is getting better all the time!

However, our form is missing something important: how spread out are the data, relative to the scale we are using? In other words, we see everything in a context. Is someone tall or short? Depends on who and where you are. A six-foot man would be tall, but not extraordinarily so. A six-foot woman is more likely to get attention in a crowd. Place that woman in Tokyo, Japan, where average heights are shorter than in the United States, and she would get a lot of attention.

If average income in a small town in the Midwest is $45,000 and there is not much variation—that is, almost everyone makes somewhere between $40,000 and $50,000—having someone move to town who makes $75,000 is a big deal. One way or another, it ends up in the corner café conversations, and invitations to serve on the local library board or to help plan the corn carnival start to arrive. Relative to the average and the spread, this income is unusual. If you had the same average income in a suburb of Chicago, where incomes easily range between $25,000 and $110,000, having someone move to the area with an income of $75,000 would not cause much of a stir.

We have already talked about the importance of understanding the central tendency of our data, where the bulk of the data lie. Now we need to understand how we measure the surrounding context, the spread of the data.

## Measures of dispersion: Standard deviation

In statistical terms, measures of spread in the data are called **measures of dispersion** and answer the question "How spread out are your data?" The most important of these measures is the **standard deviation.** The standard deviation is so important that instead of just telling you how to interpret it, we are actually going to walk through how to calculate it so you develop a true sense of what it represents.

## How spread out are your data?

### Unusual or not?

Standard deviation is an important descriptive statistic. Paired with the mean, it is how we understand whether our data are unusual. Think about it. If most of our data are all tightly clustered together and the next data point is far away from that cluster, as shown in Figure 4–1, our impulse is to say that the new data point is unusual. However, if our data are spread out widely, a new data point that is far from the center, as shown in Figure 4–2, does not seem so unusual. If you study really hard for an exam and you score 85 out of 100, you could cheer or cry; it all depends on how everyone else did and where you are relative to the rest. That, in turn, depends on whether the scores are all over the place or tightly clustered around a central place.

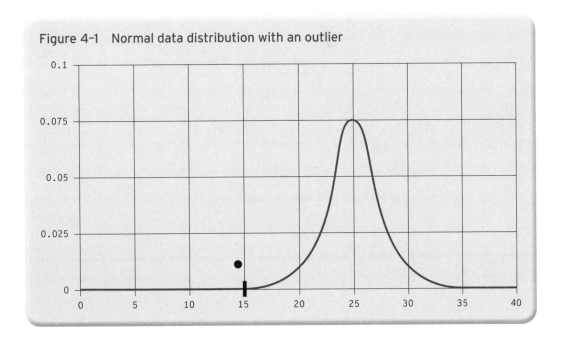

Figure 4-1   Normal data distribution with an outlier

Part of the point of descriptive statistics is to understand if a particular point is unusual or not. That is the focus of this chapter. If it is not unusual, the story ends there. If it is unusual, we will want to know if there are more "unusual points." If so, the question for the rest of the book is how to figure out if the unusual points are just scattered at random, for no particular reason, or if the unusual points are "out there" for some specific reason. But let's not get too far ahead of ourselves. Back to the benefits of first just determining if our data are tightly clustered or spread out, *dispersed*.

There are three main benefits of understanding how dispersed the data are

1. Tightly clustered data make it easier to see an outlier. Outliers are unusual. Outliers are not as clear when data are more scattered (or widely distributed).

2. The tighter the cluster of data points, the more quickly you can see a pattern, either in the bulk of the data or with outliers, if any patterns exist.

3. Seeing the dispersion in the data gives us a clue about whether the data are reliable or valid.

   • The data in Figure 4–1 may be more reliable but possibly less valid.

   • The data in Figure 4–2 may be more valid but possibly less reliable.

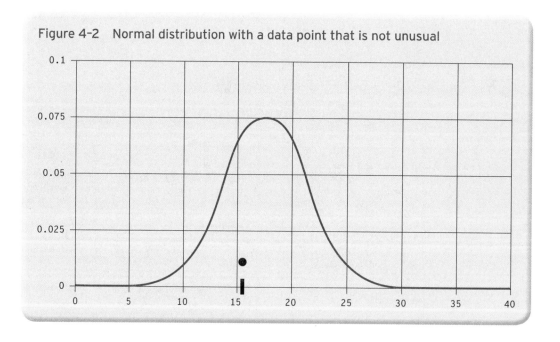

Figure 4-2    Normal distribution with a data point that is not unusual

## Average distance from the mean

So how could we measure dispersion, or spread? The term **standard deviation** should give you a clue. Most students, when asked this question, suggest that a good measure of dispersion would be the average of the distances for each point from the group average, or mean. Sounds like a good starting point. Let's use the data Nina has on per-capita debt amounts. First, let's look at Table 4–1 and identify our other descriptive statistics, the measures of central tendency: mean, median, and mode.

Table 4–1   General obligation (GO) debt per capita, 37 states, 2007

| State | GO debt per capita ($) | State | GO debt per capita ($) |
|---|---|---|---|
| Virginia | 117 | Pennsylvania | 663 |
| Missouri | 117 | Wisconsin | 704 |
| Michigan | 148 | Minnesota | 729 |
| Alabama | 167 | Vermont | 736 |
| New York | 173 | Nevada | 766 |
| Tennessee | 181 | Georgia | 806 |
| Montana | 217 | Louisiana | 896 |
| New Mexico | 227 | Mississippi | 1,074 |
| Texas | 283 | Maryland | 1,113 |
| New Jersey | 330 | California | 1,375 |
| Maine | 341 | Delaware | 1,512 |
| Arkansas | 343 | Illinois | 1,623 |
| West Virginia | 411 | Washington | 1,789 |
| Utah | 468 | Massachusetts | 2,711 |
| South Carolina | 502 | Connecticut | 3,026 |
| New Hampshire | 540 | Hawaii | 3,179 |
| Alaska | 592 | | |
| Oregon | 623 | Range | 3,062 |
| North Carolina | 651 | Mean | 823 |
| Florida | 658 | Median | 651 |
| Ohio | 661 | Mode | 117 |

The count is 37 because only 37 states recorded having general obligation (GO) debt in 2007. The state with the least amount of GO debt per capita, $117, was Virginia; the state with the highest amount, $3,179, was Hawaii. The difference between the lowest and highest is the range, or $3,062. The average, or mean, is $823. The median, or middle value, is at the nineteenth state (North Carolina) at $651. The mode, the most commonly occurring value, is $117, which occurs twice.

We can understand something about our data right away: since the mean is higher than the median, the data are skewed out to the right. In other words, we know there are some high outliers, which means there is a positive skew to the data. How do we know that? Some high values are dragging the mean over to the right of the median.

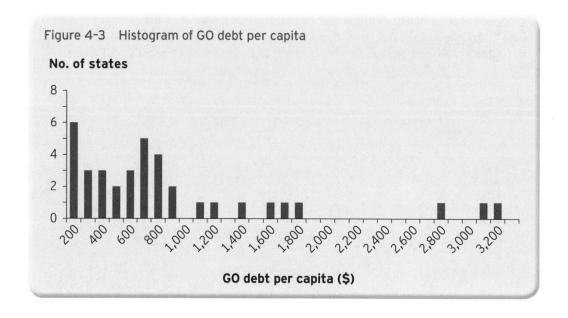

**Figure 4-3    Histogram of GO debt per capita**

What does the histogram of this data look like? A few clicks in a statistics program will show you. As you can see in Figure 4–3, most states are on the left, with GO debt per capita below $1,000. But some states have very high GO debt per capita—over $2,700! Hawaii has the most at $3,179, but Connecticut and Massachusetts are close behind at $3,026 and $2,711, respectively. With these data, we would want to use the median as a measure of central tendency, not the mean, since extreme outliers are skewing the average. In other words, the outliers are dragging the mean up to the right, making the mean pretty high relative to all the rest of the data points. If we want to understand what a typical value is, the mean would give us a false impression.

The median, or middle value, would be preferable. Would we throw out the outliers and then calculate a new mean? That is an option. In the last chapter, when we looked at house inspection data, we could throw out data for the weeks when staff was on vacation; those weeks were clearly not the norm for that department. Here, I would be more hesitant to throw out data for different states. Are these amounts clearly not the norm for these states? I am not sure. If not sure, I tend to keep the data for these states in, at least until I do more digging and find a compelling reason to toss them. Let's see what Nina does.

### Spread out or clustered?

Are the data spread out or clustered around the median? Spread out. But how spread out, really? We need the standard deviation now. Remember how we said that most students, when asked how one might measure spread, start with the average distance from each point to the mean. Okay, how do we get this? We have to calculate how far each point is from the mean (see Table 4–2), total the differences, and take the average.

But when we try to take the average of the distances, what happens? Try it. The distances total to zero! It is not surprising, actually. Since the mean is the average, it is, on average, equidistant from all the points! So our gut reaction to take the average distance from the mean is not right. At least, the calculation doesn't work. If you don't see this, try it out for yourself. But perhaps the idea is correct. . . .

Mathematicians are stubborn. If the idea is right but the calculation doesn't work, mathematicians fall back on a whole series of tricks. There are two ways to make this calculation work. The first is to take the absolute value of each number in the third column of Table 4–2. This means taking the positive and negative sign away from each. If we made each value an absolute number, added them up, and divided by the number of values, we would have the average absolute distance from the mean. Sound complicated? It is, it is hard to explain to others, and luckily, we won't use it ever again. Now that you know what it is, you can forget it.

The second way (and even more helpful) would be squaring each number so that the negatives go away. (Remember that a negative multiplied by a negative is a positive: the negatives cancel each other out.) In addition, the very high values, either positive or negative, get huge.

Of the two ways to change the data to make our original idea of "average distance to the mean" work, why do statisticians prefer this method? First, it solves the "adding up to zero" problem. Second, it gives added weight to values that are farther out. You see, part of what statisticians want to do is to emphasize that even among outliers, some are more unusual than others. Some outliers are just a little unusual, and some outliers are really, really far out there. We focus on the ones that are very unusual because we want to know *why*. We pay greater attention to points that are far from the mean because they mean that others could be far from the mean as well. We become more convinced that maybe very unusual observations are not unusual. We can illustrate the impact this has in the curves in Figures 4–4 and 4–5.

But we still need to get to the standard deviation. We are not there yet. We'll square each value as the statisticians tell us to do. If we square each value, then add them up and take the average, we have the average squared deviation from the mean. Now our squaring comes back to haunt us. Since we squared the numbers to make the calculation work in the first place, we need to unsquare what we have. In other words, we need to take the square root of the average squared deviation from the mean. And the result is, finally, the standard deviation! Whew! Aren't you glad this is a standard feature on most calculators and spreadsheets?

When we put measures of central tendency and measures of dispersion together, we have a great idea of what our data look like. In fact, used together, we can tell whether our data are tightly clustered.

Table 4–2   Distance from each point to the mean

| State | GO debt per capita ($) | Mean ($) | Distance from point to mean ($) |
|---|---|---|---|
| Virginia | 117 | 823 | 706 |
| Missouri | 117 | 823 | 706 |
| Michigan | 148 | 823 | 675 |
| Alabama | 167 | 823 | 656 |
| New York | 173 | 823 | 650 |
| Tennessee | 181 | 823 | 642 |
| Montana | 217 | 823 | 606 |
| New Mexico | 227 | 823 | 596 |
| Texas | 283 | 823 | 540 |
| New Jersey | 330 | 823 | 493 |
| Maine | 341 | 823 | 482 |
| Arkansas | 343 | 823 | 480 |
| West Virginia | 411 | 823 | 412 |
| Utah | 468 | 823 | 355 |
| South Carolina | 502 | 823 | 321 |
| New Hampshire | 540 | 823 | 283 |
| Alaska | 592 | 823 | 231 |
| Oregon | 623 | 823 | 200 |
| North Carolina | 651 | 823 | 172 |
| Florida | 658 | 823 | 165 |
| Ohio | 661 | 823 | 162 |
| Pennsylvania | 663 | 823 | 160 |
| Wisconsin | 704 | 823 | 119 |
| Minnesota | 729 | 823 | 94 |
| Vermont | 736 | 823 | 87 |
| Nevada | 766 | 823 | 57 |
| Georgia | 806 | 823 | 17 |
| Louisiana | 896 | 823 | -73 |
| Mississippi | 1,074 | 823 | -251 |
| Maryland | 1,113 | 823 | -290 |
| California | 1,375 | 823 | -552 |
| Delaware | 1,512 | 823 | -689 |
| Illinois | 1,623 | 823 | -800 |
| Washington | 1,789 | 823 | -966 |
| Massachusetts | 2,711 | 823 | -1,888 |
| Connecticut | 3,026 | 823 | -2,203 |
| Hawaii | 3,179 | 823 | -2,356 |

- If the standard deviation is large relative to the mean, the data are widely spread out.
- If the standard deviation is small relative to the mean, the data are tightly clustered.

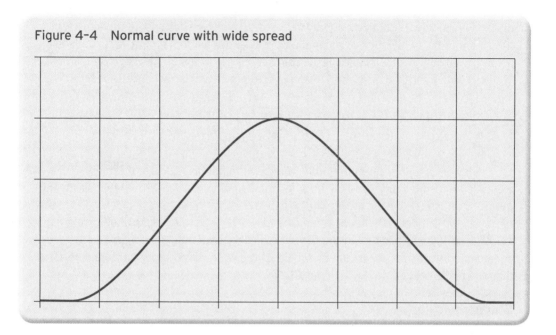

Figure 4-4    Normal curve with wide spread

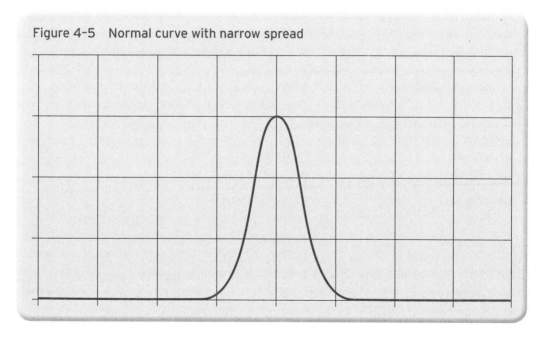

Figure 4-5    Normal curve with narrow spread

For example, if in one data set the mean per capita GO debt is $823 and the standard deviation is $8, the data are going to be clustered very tightly around $823. If in another data set, the mean per-capita GO debt is $823 and the standard deviation is $300, the data will be very spread out. In both cases, the mean is the same, but the standard deviation is different. But think about it: if we only had the values for standard deviation, without the benchmark of the mean or median (either will do but we usually use mean), we would not be able to tell anything about the forms of the curves of the data. We need both a measure of central tendency and a measure of dispersion.

> Standard deviation means nothing just by itself. You have to look at it with the mean or median.

Standard deviation is important only in relation to the overall data. If I told you that in a data set hidden behind my back the standard deviation was 7.5, would that mean anything? No. It would only be meaningful if you knew that the mean was 750 or 75. In the first case, the standard deviation would be small compared to the mean, indicating that the data are tightly clustered. In the second case, the standard deviation would be large compared to the mean, indicating that the data are widely spread out or more spread out than the first case. Let's go back to our GO debt per-capita table (now Table 4–3).

### Standard deviation

We now know that the standard deviation is the square root of the average of the squared distances from the mean—in this case, $765. It's important to note that just as outliers can skew the mean and thus the general or true pattern of the data, they can also affect the standard deviation and skew the general pattern or overall distribution of the data in a similar way. To illustrate this, let's take out the three high states (Massachusetts, Connecticut, and Hawaii), and see what happens. Our standard deviation drops to $475! This means that these three states are outliers; that is, they are different from the general pattern of the rest of the states. Their extremely high values make the overall distribution much wider—in other words, make the standard deviation much larger. In practical use, Nina may want to exclude these three states from her analysis because their unusual values may be masking the pattern that describes the overall data set much better.

As you can see, standard deviation is a very powerful tool. If you have a data set, no matter how large, you can calculate the mean and the standard deviation, as well as many, many other more-complicated statistical values, with a few simple keystrokes in any spreadsheet program. The spreadsheet programs have preprogrammed formulas for any statistic you need, so you can find exactly where any data point is relative to all the other points! Well, I realize this fact may not thrill you, but it is very, very useful in understanding data and doing research. In fact, almost all efforts made to prove something—that a particular medicine works, that military strategy

**Table 4-3**     Distance from each point to the mean, squared, totaled, averaged, and square-rooted (whew!)

| State | GO debt per capita ($) | Mean ($) | Distance from point to mean ($) | Distance from point to mean, squared ($) |
|---|---|---|---|---|
| Virginia | 117 | 823 | 706 | 498,436 |
| Missouri | 117 | 823 | 706 | 498,436 |
| Michigan | 148 | 823 | 675 | 455,625 |
| Alabama | 167 | 823 | 656 | 430,336 |
| New York | 173 | 823 | 650 | 422,500 |
| Tennessee | 181 | 823 | 642 | 412,164 |
| Montana | 217 | 823 | 606 | 367,236 |
| New Mexico | 227 | 823 | 596 | 355,216 |
| Texas | 283 | 823 | 540 | 291,600 |
| New Jersey | 330 | 823 | 493 | 243,049 |
| Maine | 341 | 823 | 482 | 232,324 |
| Arkansas | 343 | 823 | 480 | 230,400 |
| West Virginia | 411 | 823 | 412 | 169,744 |
| Utah | 468 | 823 | 355 | 126,025 |
| South Carolina | 502 | 823 | 321 | 103,041 |
| New Hampshire | 540 | 823 | 283 | 80,089 |
| Alaska | 592 | 823 | 231 | 53,361 |
| Oregon | 623 | 823 | 200 | 40,000 |
| North Carolina | 651 | 823 | 172 | 29,584 |
| Florida | 658 | 823 | 165 | 27,225 |
| Ohio | 661 | 823 | 162 | 26,244 |
| Pennsylvania | 663 | 823 | 160 | 25,600 |
| Wisconsin | 704 | 823 | 119 | 14,161 |
| Minnesota | 729 | 823 | 94 | 8,836 |
| Vermont | 736 | 823 | 87 | 7,569 |
| Nevada | 766 | 823 | 57 | 3,249 |
| Georgia | 806 | 823 | 17 | 289 |
| Louisiana | 896 | 823 | -73 | 5,329 |
| Mississippi | 1,074 | 823 | -251 | 63,001 |
| Maryland | 1,113 | 823 | -290 | 84,100 |
| California | 1,375 | 823 | -552 | 304,704 |
| Delaware | 1,512 | 823 | -689 | 474,721 |
| Illinois | 1,623 | 823 | -800 | 640,000 |
| Washington | 1,789 | 823 | -966 | 933,156 |
| Massachusetts | 2,711 | 823 | -1,888 | 3,564,544 |
| Connecticut | 3,026 | 823 | -2,203 | 4,853,209 |
| Hawaii | 3,179 | 823 | -2,356 | 5,550,736 |
| Total | | | | 21,625,839 |
| Average squared deviation | | | | 584,482 |
| Square root of average squared deviation of the mean | | | | 765 |

protects a population, or that someone committed a crime—rely on means and standard deviations and the topic of our next section, normal curves.

Whoa! We have talked about means and standard deviations, and a little about normal curves (remember Figure 3–6?), but not about how they all work together. Enter the beauty of the $z$-scores and the central limit theorem.

## Normal curves

All statisticians will tell you that a normal curve is beautiful. It is shapely, even, and smooth, and looks like a bell. It is symmetrical. It is beautiful because, as shown in Figure 4–6, certain mathematical rules exist for all normal curves, allowing them to serve as a measuring stick of sorts:

- Of all data points, 68% fall within one standard deviation of the mean.
- Of all data points, 95% fall within two standard deviations of the mean.
- Of all data points, 99.9% fall within three standard deviations of the mean.

What does this mean? If you have a complete data set, you have all the data points. If you put these points on a graph, you have a distribution. So if you put a

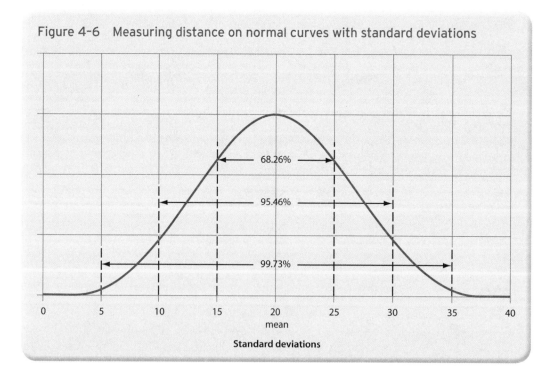

Figure 4-6    Measuring distance on normal curves with standard deviations

normal curve over this data set, it will cover all the data points. Still following me? You can then take any point on that normal curve, and there will be some portion of the curve (percentage), below that data point, that goes all the way down to the lower end. There will also be some portion (percentage) of the curve, above that data point, that goes all the way to the highest end. (Note that with a normal curve, the ends go out to infinity, so you would never quite reach 100% and you would never reach 0%).

Where am I going with this? All data sets, and therefore all normal curves, follow these same rules. The beauty of the standard deviation is that it serves as *a standard measuring stick for us to use with any and every data set. If you know the mean and the standard deviation of a data set,* you can find where any value is, from the lowest point to the upper point, on the normal curve. You can do this by measuring, in standard deviations, and then by percentages, how far that data point is from the mean.

> If you know the mean and the standard deviation of a data set, you can find where any value is.

Using the measuring stick, I'll illustrate. If we have a normal curve, with a mean of 20 and a standard deviation of 5, I know the following mathematical facts (just using the same rules already listed, with 20 inserted for the mean and 5 inserted for the standard deviation):

- Of all data points, 68% fall within one standard deviation (5) of the mean (20).
- Of all data points, 95% fall within two standard deviations (2 times 5, or 10) of the mean (20).
- Of all data points, 99.9% fall within three standard deviations (3 times 5, or 15) of the mean (20).

I can fill in the numbers like this:

- Of all data points, 68% fall within the value of 20 +/– 5.
- Of all data points, 95% fall within the value of 20 +/– 10.
- Of all data points, 99.9% fall within the value of 20 +/– 15.

Then I can fill in the numbers even more completely like this:

- Of all data points, 68% fall between the values of 15 and 25.
- Of all data points, 95% fall between the values of 10 and 30.
- Of all data points, 99.5% fall between 5 and 35.

Because the percentages under any curve must add up to 100%. In the example above, almost 100% of the points are between 5 and 35, the points that are each three standard deviations from the mean. We also know that if one portion of the curve falls between two numbers on either side of the center, the rest of the curve has to be below and above those numbers. And since the normal curve is symmetrical, whatever is left has to be split between the low end and the high end, in the two "tails." With our example, as seen in Figure 4–6, this means that

- If 68% of all data points fall between the values of 15 and 25, then the rest, 32%, are split between values below 15 or above 25. So 16% of the values in the data set are below 15 and 16% of them are above 25.

- If 95% of all data points fall between the values of 10 and 30, then the rest, or 5%, are split between values below 10 and above 30. So 2.5% of the values in the data set are below 10 and 2.5% are above 30.

- If 99.9% of all data points fall between 5 and 35, then the rest (or only 0.01%) are split between values below 5 and above 35. Therefore, 0.5% of the values in the data set are below 5 and 0.5% are above 35.

These facts are the same whether you have a hundred data points in your data set or a million. Right away, if you give me any number, I can tell you about where it falls in my example data set. What about the data point 42? I know 42 is really high,

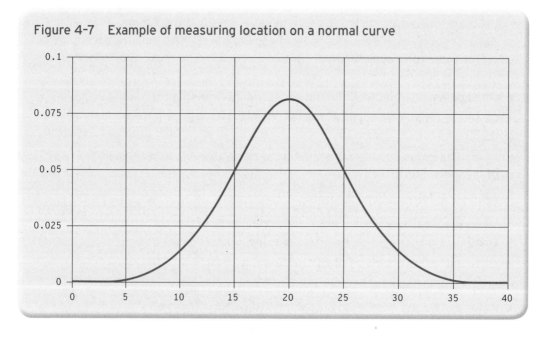

Figure 4-7   Example of measuring location on a normal curve

relative to the rest of the data. In fact, I know it is somewhere between the 99.9th and 100th percentiles. I can't get all the way to 100%, of course, but the data point 42 is somewhere in the teeny-tiny tail. What about 8? It is somewhere in the bottom 16th percentile. Try 18. I know right away that it is just below the 50% mark (the mean is 20), not even one standard deviation away from the mean.

## The z-score

I illustrated with some examples how using standard deviations and a normal curve worked. We learned we could know where every point is by using our measuring stick of standard deviations. Statisticians call this the **z-score.** The z-score is the number of standard deviations a particular point is away from the mean in a data set. If I know the mean and the standard deviation, I can calculate a z-score for any number in any normally distributed data set. I use the following formula:

$$z = \frac{(\text{data point} - \text{mean})}{\text{standard deviation}}$$

*[handwritten: $4 - 7 = \frac{-3}{1.5}$]*

*[handwritten: $-2$]*

   Again, the z-score is just a fancy way to measure the distance between the data point and the mean using our measuring stick of standard deviations. What is cool is that this tool lets us work backward: by knowing the z-score, I know right away about where the data point is relative to the rest of the data set. With a z-score that is +/– 2 or more, I know my data point is somewhere in the upper or lower tail of the data set. If the z-score is –2 or lower, my data point is in the bottom 2.5% of the curve and almost all the other data points are above it. If the z-score is +2 or higher, my data point is in the top 2.5% of the curve and almost all the data points are below it.
   Let's illustrate how z-scores work with a couple of examples:
   Example #1: We could consider how a local government such as Council Top compares to others in the state in terms of police response time. The tricky part of this example is that we would want the response time to be low, meaning that police are arriving quickly. Let's say the average response time across the state is 7.0 minutes. The wonderful spreadsheet program Nina is using calculates the standard deviation of the data set for her, and it is 1.5 minutes. What if Council Top's response time is only 4.0 minutes? Apply these numbers to the formula for z-scores. The difference between our data point and the average is 3.0 minutes. We divide this by the standard deviation, or 1.5 minutes. Council Top's data point has a z-score of –2; in other words, it is two standard deviations below the average. Only 2.5% of jurisdictions have a lower response time than Council Top. Almost all the other jurisdictions have higher average response times. This tells us that our community is doing well compared to others in the state. The police officers (and the staff in the public safety call center, and the mechanics, and the support staff) all should get a raise.
   Example #2: To see how our community is doing in terms of education, we can look at a data set of standardized test scores in the state, county, or even grade level. For instance, if we look at elementary schools across the state and our community has a z-score of 1, it means that our school's scores are one standard deviation above the mean. This tells us that our community is doing well but has room to improve. To be at the top of the state in terms of scores, we would want to be two standard deviations above the mean. This would put us in the top 2.5% in the state.

### Z-scores: Population or sample?

There are two important points to remember about using z-scores. First, when applying the z-score formula, you need to use the mean and standard deviation either

(1) for a population (if you have observations for a full population; for every individual unit, such as all fifty states; all people in the municipality; or all students in a school) or

(2) for a sample (such as a subset of states; a sample of people in the municipality; or a sample of students in each grade).

As I pointed out previously, the calculation for standard deviation is slightly different for a sample than it is for a population. (The difference between **population** and **sample** is discussed further in Chapter 6.)

Even though we went through the calculation for standard deviation, my assumption is that you will not be calculating a standard deviation by hand but will use a spreadsheet. Make sure that you use the appropriate formula.

> The calculation for standard deviation is slightly different for a sample than it is for a population. Choose the appropriate one when using the formula in a spreadsheet.

Second, we need to assume that the curve is normal—in other words, that the data are normally distributed in the form of a bell-shaped curve. All the z-scores and accompanying percentages under the curve, such as 95% of the observations falling within two standard deviations of the mean, are based on a bell-shaped curve. If we do not have a bell-shaped-curve distribution, in theory, we can't use z-scores.

Well, you might think, "Okay, if this is true, this is really, really helpful. *Not* [said in a sarcastic voice]. How often do normal curves just appear in data in real life?" Luckily, more often than you think. For example, imagine the heights of all the people in your town. Some are tall. A few are very tall. Some are short. A few are very short. But most fall in between. With thousands of observations, the distribution of heights across an entire city usually falls onto a normal curve. This same phenomenon appears with many other characteristics in nature.

More importantly, we can still use z-scores with almost any set of sample data, even if the population distribution is skewed. But wait, I just said, two paragraphs above, that z-scores can only be used with a normal curve! So how can both be true? Let me explain. We can assume everything has a normal distribution because of the beauty of the central limit theorem.

### The central limit theorem

The distribution of averages tends to be normal, even when the distribution from which the averages are computed is not.

Another way to say this is:

> The distribution of averages of samples tends to be normal, even when the distribution of the entire data set from which the samples are taken is not.

Huh?

We often encounter skewed distributions in statistics. Think back to my discussion in Chapter 1 of Michael Jordan's income being very high for geography major graduates at the University of North Carolina at Chapel Hill, and the discussion of how a high value can skew a distribution in Chapter 3. This is the case when I look at all geography majors, the whole population. But if I take a sample of geography majors, Michael is not likely to be in the sample. If I take another sample, he is not likely to be in that sample, either. (There are many geography majors over the years, and only one Michael Jordan.) If I take the average of each of these samples and plot these on a histogram, I have a distribution of averages. I can do this repeatedly. Maybe one of these samples will include Michael Jordan and that particular average will be skewed, but otherwise, I have mostly nonskewed averages. The distribution of all these sample averages is normal.

## There is only one Michael Jordan.

This phenomenon allows us to assume normality with almost all applied statistics calculations. I will say it again because it is important. There is only one Michael Jordan (and he went to the University of North Carolina [UNC] at Chapel Hill, in case you forgot). But just because his salary skews the distribution of incomes of geography majors, it will not skew the vast majority of samples taken from all geography majors. In fact, it is so unlikely to get Michael Jordon in a sample that, for simplicity's sake, we can just assume that none of the samples will be skewed. While this may seem like sacrilege to a UNC professor like me, I am going to ignore Michael Jordon. We can assume all samples fit a normal curve. So if you are using statistics with a sample and someone questions your work because there are some outliers in the population, you can simply refer to the central limit theorem and watch their eyes glaze over.

## We generally get to assume our data are normally distributed, which makes life sooo much easier!

In the next several chapters, we'll discuss how probabilities, normal curves, standard deviations, and *z*-scores set the stage for inferential statistics, where we are no longer describing a population but trying to infer something about a population from just a sample.

Onward!

Are Your Property Taxes Fair?
An Application of Descriptive Statistics: The Coefficient of Dispersion[1]

Property taxes are a major source of funding for local governments, and are often the focus of citizen scrutiny. One of the most important aspects of any tax, but particularly the property tax, is fairness. The property tax is based on the appraised value of the property in question. The appraised value should represent government's best estimate of the value of the property. How do we know if the government is making a good estimate of fair market value for properties, and therefore is applying the property tax fairly?

We can measure the fair market value directly when a property is bought or sold. The government is doing a good job in estimating value if the assessed value is close to the market value as shown by the selling price. This is easy to see with one or two houses, but we need something to tell us if the government is doing a good job in assessments over all. So periodically local governments calculate what is called the assessment-to-sales ratio, or simply "sales ratio," which is the ratio of the appraisals of various properties to the actual prices for those properties when sales occur. To understand how well the city is doing overall, it calculates an overall assessment ratio, which is the assessed value of all properties that have sold and are valid, arms-length transactions in the jurisdiction divided by estimated fair market value (sometimes called equalized value) of all properties. This allows jurisdictions to compare themselves with how they are doing overall to other jurisdictions.

Of course, you want to be as accurate as possible overall, but 100% accuracy will never happen. Market conditions can change rapidly, the assessors may make errors, or certain sales can be quirky. It is understood that some assessments will be off by a little, and some will be off by a lot. For example, if the assessment ratio is 90% it would mean that, on average, properties are assessed at 90% of actual market value based on sales. If everyone's property is assessed at 90% of value, the assessments are inaccurate, but everyone is treated the same. If, however, one property is assessed at 80% and another property is assessed at 100%, the average assessment ratio is also 90%, but the two properties are treated very differently.

To test the fairness of assessments, local governments use a second measure to understand how consistently they in measuring the value of a property subject to property tax in its jurisdiction; this is the coefficient of dispersion (COD).

In simple terms, the COD is a measure of the spread of all the assessment ratios around the median assessment ratio. Again, assessments are never going to be entirely accurate, although some jurisdictions would love to have assessment-to-sales ratios of 0.95 or 0.98 all the time! But if you lay out all of the assessment ratios and look at the distribution around the median, if there is a wide spread, or dispersion, it means some of the assessments are way off.

Here is how a national expert on property assessment describes it:

"The COD is a measure of how close (or far) from your median assessment level you are on average." An example is a property that sells for $100,000 and the assessor values it at $90,000. The assessment-to-sales ratio for this property is 90,000/100,000 or 90% or 0.9.

To determine the COD, you take all of the assessment ratios measured during your measurement period (typically during the previous year) and determine your median. The COD is then a simple calculation moving forward. Let's say you have seven ratios in your set and they are 0.70, 0.75, 0.84, 0.92, 0.95, 0.99, and 1.04. You then calculate the absolute value of each from the median. (As a reminder, absolute values means we ignore + or –.) In this example, the median is 0.92.

$$0.70 - 0.92 = 0.22$$
$$0.75 - 0.92 = 0.17$$
$$0.84 - 0.92 = 0.08$$
$$0.92 - 0.92 = 0.00$$
$$0.95 - 0.92 = 0.03$$
$$0.99 - 0.92 = 0.07$$
$$1.04 - 0.92 = 0.12$$

Each of these absolute differences tells us how far each individual ratio is from the median. (As a reminder, absolute values means we ignore + or –.)  You then add all of the differences together:

$$0.22 + 0.17 + 0.08 + 0.00 + 0.03 + 0.07 + 0.12 = 0.690.$$

Take the total absolute differences number and divide it by the total items in your set. In this example it would be

$$0.69/7 = 0.09857$$

The 0.09857 is the average absolute deviation (ADD).

You then convert this to a percent by dividing the AAD by the median and multiplying by 100. In this case it is

$$(0.09857/0.92) \times 100 = 10.71$$

The COD in this example is 10.71. So in this example, you would say that assessment value in this example town is, in general, between 10% and 11% off. Average assessment ratio. With an average assessment value of 90%, the range in this example would be between 79% and 101%. A low COD means greater consistency between assessment and more fairness in assessment. A COD of 15% or below is a common benchmark.

1.  Thank you to Kenneth Joyner, lecturer in public finance and government. Kenneth is a former tax assessor. Among other positions, he formally chaired the Uniform Standards of Professional Appraisal Practice and Appraiser Regulatory Committee of the International Association of Assessing Officers (IAAO), and he currently serves on the IAAO executive board. Thanks also to David Ammons, Albert Coates, professor of public administration and government and author of *Municipal Benchmarks: Assessing Local Performance and Establishing Community Standards*. Both David and Kenneth are on the faculty at the School of Government, University of North Carolina at Chapel Hill.

## "So even though we seem to be far above the average in terms of

our GO debt per capita, we are really not that unusual?" The council member sounded surprised.

" "Yes, ma'am. The data are really spread out. While the bulk of the data are here," Nina pointed to the figure on the PowerPoint slide, "there are a number of states with low GO debt and several with very high GO debt. In fact, it is only when you look at what the debt is used for that we can get some good comparisons."

"Well, can we do that?"

"I already did. If you look at this next slide, you'll see the ten other states that are using GO debt in the same way that we are. We are right in the middle, close to the median, in terms of our per-capita debt levels."

"So do you feel that we can increase our debt without any problem?" asked the chair.

"I didn't say that. That is a different question. I can say that we are not unusual," Nina said with a slight smile.

## Review questions

1. What is a standard deviation, and what is its purpose?

2. If the mean in a data set is higher than the median, what does this indicate about the data?

3. Define *central limit theorem*. Explain why the mean, median, and mode would be the same value in a normal distribution.

4. What does a *z*-score represent? If someone told you that a data point in a data set has the *z*-score of +2, what could you assume?

5. Why can we assume that most data sets are normally distributed?

6. How can we use a *z*-score if the data set is not normally distributed?

7. How might your own local government use a *z*-score to examine its efficiency or effectiveness?

8. What data would you need for your example in #7?

9. In your example, what *z*-score would you want the data set representing your community to have?

10. Explain how this could be true: "The distribution of an average tends to be normal, even when the distribution from which the average is computed is not."

# How Much Is Not Much?

## 5

[ PROBABILITY ]

**Chuck was happy.** He had already prepared the agenda for Monday night's meeting, which held nothing particularly controversial; the weekend was supposed to be sunny, and his golf clubs were waiting. Only a few hours to go on a beautiful Friday afternoon until five o'clock.

Then he sighed. What an illusion. As city manager, he was never really off the clock. Last weekend it was the grand opening of the new animal shelter. This weekend, although nothing was scheduled, that didn't mean he wouldn't get a call about a spill at the sewage plant or a house with forty pit bulls discovered in it. He chuckled. That had actually happened in the next county, and he and all the other surrounding jurisdictions had to provide space for the pit bulls because the county shelter couldn't handle them all. And there might have been more dogs, but neighbors stopped by and some dogs "disappeared" as soon as the notice started going out on police scanners. What a mess. Oh well, he could at least hope for a calm weekend.

Chuck spent another two hours reviewing the town's personnel policies. If anything was going to be controversial in the coming week, it was going to be whether to expand the volunteer firefighter force or to hire another career firefighter. The phone rang.

"Chuck, did you hear the news about Red Oak?" Red Oak was not the local baseball team; it was a small community to the northeast of Council Top, along the river. The caller was John Vernon, a friend who was a retired firefighter. John listened to the emergency medical services scanner all the time, following what happened where over the whole region.

"No, what's up, John?"

"There's a fire at the old Stanley Furniture store on Route 5 going out of town. It is still burning; probably will for days. The place was packed with furniture that the owners were going to sell at an auction at the end of the month."

"Oh, geez. Sounds like it would take four or five crews."

"There's more: the roof collapsed about a half hour ago, with three guys inside. Two are out, but one is missing."

"Oh, no." Chuck was quiet for a moment.

"Yeah."

"You know this stuff, John. What's the chance he'll be found?"

"After a half hour, not much, based on my experience."

"Red Oak is an all-volunteer force, isn't it?"

"Yep, from what I know, the initial crew response was volunteers. I don't know which other crews from neighboring towns are there now."

"I'd better talk to our fire chief to see about what support efforts are going on. Thanks for letting me know, John."

"Sure, Chuck. I'll talk to you later."

The day didn't seem so sunny anymore. Chuck started making phone calls, wondering what "not much" meant in terms of probability.

The topic that most seems to scare students in public administration research methods is **probability**. But to move from descriptive statistics to inferential statistics, we need to understand probability. More specifically, we need to understand how probability relates to how confident we can be with our conclusions and how we identify random or purposeful patterns in the data. Take time with this material. There are no big formulas and not a lot of numbers, but the concepts are at the heart of the rest of the book.

Up to this point we have primarily focused on descriptive statistics. You may recall that descriptive statistics simply describe the data we have in hand. We cannot make larger generalizations about the world; we can only describe what is right in front of us. It is what it is. There is no chance involved, no error other than human error in measuring the data or in calculating the descriptive statistic value.

And, up to this point, we have not had to distinguish between a population and a sample. A *population of data* is data from all of our units of analysis. For example, we are taking data from all 50 states, or all the schools in the county, or all the police officers on the force, or all the fire truck crews, or all the employees. The key word is *all*. When we calculate descriptive statistics on a population, we include every person, everything, or every place. There is no guesswork or estimates. It is what it is. When we calculate the mean, we can be exact, and there is no question we are correct (as long as we did the math right!).

Inferential statistics are different.

## Inferential statistics: Using a sample

With inferential statistics we try to infer something about the broader world from a sample of data. For example, we could not know exactly what the average income is in the city of Seattle unless we asked every single person earning a living in the city what his or her income is—and even then, our answer probably would not be accurate because some people would lie. In addition, the value would change the next day, since someone would quit a job, someone else would be hired, someone else would die, and someone else would get a raise.

When you have a relatively small number of data points, or observations, in a population, you can go ahead and gather information for every unit; for example, you could gather data for all fifty states since all fifty states is a population. You might be able to get data on income for a population if all you want to know is the exact average income on your street, because usually there are not that many people on a single street. It is possible to go to each house and ask. But with most research questions, the population is much larger, and we cannot possibly ask every single person, or survey every single house, or observe every single classroom, or test every single student.

So we take a sample. And we hope this sample is a good representation of the larger whole. In other words, we hope that from the sample, we can infer something about the larger population. This is where probability comes in. Either it is very likely that the sample is a good representation of the population, or it is not very likely. It is very probable, or it is not very probable. There is a good chance of the sample being representative, or there is not a good chance.

> Is the sample a good representation of the population?
> Ah, Watson, that is the question!

## Likelihood, probability, chance

What is the *likelihood*, the *probability*, the *chance* of something happening? I use these terms interchangeably, not to give you a headache but to make you realize that these terms mean the same thing. Working with data in cities and counties commonly uses all three.

Recently, Sean, a former student, told me that certain parts of statistics suddenly "clicked" with him when he realized that they applied to his work in Iraq. He was part of a team in charge of a roadblock in Iraq, and they noticed that when it rained, they discovered much larger caches of weapons in vehicles. The question he asked was, "Was this random luck at my post, or was it representative of all roadblocks in Iraq?" He did not actually do the calculations, but he understood how he could apply statistics to that question. He wanted to know if the sample of cars at his one roadblock was representative of the whole population of cars stopped at roadblocks in Iraq. The material in this chapter will help you answer this type of question.

Are two things related? In Sean's case, were insurgents trying to pass through more weapons in certain weather conditions? Were rain and weapons transfers related? We cannot know that for sure, but we can try to assess how likely it is.

***Related, or not related.***     Of course, statistics professors have to make it more complicated. Instead of just checking to see how likely it is that two things are related, we approach the question by asking how likely it is that the two things are *un*related. In other words, how likely is it that someone would see the data you have, such as finding a lot of cars with weapons during rainstorms, if there were no relationship? Was it just by chance that, during rainstorms, many people who were stopped had weapons?

These two questions fit together, of course. The probability of any event can only go up to 100%. That 100% can be broken into the probability of two things *being related* and the probability of two things *not being related*. Together, these two must add up to 100%. As the probability of two things being related goes up, the probability of the same two things *not* being related goes down. If the probability of two things being related goes down, the probability of the same two things *not* being related goes up. If two things are *not* really related, any pattern we might see between them is random. Remember this: "not related" means that any patterns are random.

## Anything can be random.

I must stop here and state a fact, a rule, something that—even if it is hard to believe—you must accept as a scientist: *Anything* can be random. *Nothing* is certain. *Nothing* can be proven. We cannot be completely confident in any result. There is no total, absolute confidence in two things being related or unrelated. We might be very, very confident—even 99.9% sure—but there is always a chance that the data we have are the result of random chance. For example, while very, very improbable, you could flip a coin a million times and get "heads" every time. It is *possible;* it's just not probable.

## Confidence

This is where the concept of *confidence* comes in. As I pointed out earlier in this chapter, there is always a very small, tiny, infinitesimal chance that the sample data you have are not representative of the population, or that two groups of data are not related even when it looks as though they are.

Let me explain. We want to know if our sample data are a good snapshot of the "truth"; if there is a pattern in the population, we want to see a pattern in the survey data. If there is no pattern in the population, we want to see no pattern in the survey data.

While we hope the sample data are a true reflection of the population, there is always a possibility that just by random chance we came up with a sample that is not a good reflection of the population: a bad sample. We can try to minimize this happening, but we can't totally eliminate the possibility of a bad sample. So we try to understand the likelihood of getting a bad sample, one that doesn't show the true nature of the population. This is where you see a pattern in the sample when in truth there is not a distinct and meaningful pattern in the population. Instead, the pattern in the survey data was due to just random chance.

For example, you might have response rate data for a sample of volunteer fire departments over ten years in the north part of a state, and similar data for a sample of volunteer fire departments in the south. When plotted out, it looks like the northern departments have lowered the response times in the past three years, while the southern ones have held steady. You may in fact have a pattern showing true improvement in the north and none in the south. Or you may not; you may have just pulled, at random, a couple of departments in the north with lower response times.

Conversely, perhaps your sample doesn't show any interesting pattern, while in truth there is a clear and important pattern in the population. Your sample just happened, by random chance, to miss it. To go back to the volunteer fire department example, let's say the northern departments have consistently lowered their response times by implementing a new collaborative call center system with the area sheriff's departments. Of course, there are a couple of exceptions. If your sample had several of the higher response time "exceptions" in it, just by random chance, you might miss a pattern of true improvement.

If the chance of the sample data being bad is very, very low—say, 5% or lower—and you see a pattern linking two groups of data, you can say with confidence that the survey data are a *valid* representation of the population or that the two groups of data are related. If the chance of the sample data being bad is higher—say, 20% or 30%—you would not be as confident in saying that there is a relationship.

***Patterns in data.***    How do we understand whether there is a small chance or a large chance that the data are random? Do your data seem unusual given other data or what is known of the situation, or do they seem to fit? Trust your instincts first. If the result is not what you expected, you should look at everything a second time. If something looks wrong, it probably is.

Then you look at how clear the patterns (or lack of patterns) are. If you plot the data points on a graph and it looks just like my two-year-old's picture of snow falling, you can be confident there is not a true pattern hiding in the data. In the same vein, if there is a clear, direct pattern in the data—like a straight line trending upward between my kids' ages and their requests for money, increasing in tandem—we are more confident in saying there is a relationship between two things. To take a more serious example, we can go back to the question of a relationship between weather and weapons: If the number of weapons found *always* goes up when it rains, I would be confident that there is a relationship between the two. If it only happened *sometimes*, I would be less confident that there is a relationship between them.

Sample data, probability, and confidence: statistics brings these all together to help us draw conclusions. First, you look at the data and see what it seems to show (or not to show). Then you think about the probability that the sample is giving you the wrong picture. That leads you then to how confident you are in your conclusion.

We have already talked about data. We will revisit the ideas of probability and confidence multiple times here and in the coming chapters. The practical lesson to this section is not to trust someone who wants to draw a conclusion based on just a few observations, claiming there is a pattern. Argue that you are not *confident* in the results, because there is too high a *probability* that these few *data* points are just *random*. Then your friends will be so impressed they will buy you a beer. Or, more likely, they will edge away slowly, suddenly remembering they had promised the spouse that they would clean out the garage today.

## Basic law of probability

There are two important terms to understand when you speak of probability: an **event** and an **outcome.** An event might be easily described as something that happens that can have multiple outcomes—for example, when a choice is made, when something changes, or when a separation into different groups takes place. It could be a very small, minute choice, such as deciding what socks to wear on a particular day, or a major occurrence, such as giving birth to a child. The outcome is what results: you wear blue socks or the new addition to your family is a boy.

The basic law of probability is as follows:

$$\frac{\text{The number of ways that a particular outcome can happen}}{\text{The number of ways that all possible outcomes can happen}} = \text{Probability.}$$

In a way, probability is just working with fractions, knowing what goes on top and what goes on the bottom. The best example, and one that is used repeatedly, is the infamous coin flip. If you have a coin (assuming it is legitimate and not rigged), and you flip it 100 times, you will get heads about half the time and tails about half the time. Okay, I realize that this statement will prompt some smart aleck out there to actually flip a coin 100 times just to test that statement, and he or she will actually get 54 heads and 46 tails, or 53 heads and 47 tails, or 35 heads and 65 tails. But I assure you, if 100 people flipped the coin, on average, one-half of the flips would be heads and one-half of the flips would be tails. This is how probabilities are determined. Each flip is an event. There are two possible outcomes. In the end, if you could flip a coin 100 times repeatedly and repeatedly, millions of times, the number of times that heads would come up is, on average, 50 out of 100 flips.

## A probability is just a fraction.

What is the probability of seeing a boy when you first lay eyes on a newborn child? We know, over the long run—over about a couple of billion "events" over the course of history—that there is about a 51% chance of having a boy and about a 49% chance of having a girl. (We suspect that since girls are slightly more likely to survive to age one and live longer on average, nature gives boys a fighting chance by giving them the birth edge.)

Fortunately, we can figure out probabilities in another way, too. What is the probability of you wearing blue socks tomorrow? Depends on how many blue socks, and socks of other colors, are in your drawer when you are making the decision (the event). If all my socks are blue, there is a 100% chance that, if I wear a pair of my socks (the event), the socks will be blue (the outcome). If only one pair of socks is blue and 99 pairs are black, my chance of picking the blue pair is one out of 100, or 1%. Let's say I have only 25 pairs of socks. If 5 pairs of socks are blue, and the remaining 20 pairs are black, then my chance of picking a blue pair is 5/25, or 1/5, or 20%. Another example: if there are 100 students in a room, 25 of them women and 75 of them men, and I pick one at random (the event), the probability of picking a woman is 25/100 or 1/4, or 25% (the outcome).

### The language of probabilities

These probabilities are easy. But life is never easy, and local government management is only slightly less complicated than life. How do we determine probabilities that are more complex and use them for decision-making? We need to use some basic rules to let us learn the language of probabilities.

Rule 1: something must happen. That is, if an outcome is possible, there is a probability associated with it. In a simple but happy example, with the event of having a healthy baby there are two possible outcomes: (1) having a new baby boy or (2) having a new baby girl.

Rule 2: The probabilities of all possible outcomes added together equals 1. If you add up the probability of having a girl and the probability of having a boy, you have all possible outcomes, and 100% of the probability:

Probability of boy + probability of girl = 100%.

Rule 3: This means that if we know the probability of one outcome happening, we also know the probability that that particular outcome will *not* happen. When there are only two possible outcomes, we know that if one outcome does not occur, the other outcome will. Thus, if I know the probability of having a girl (49%), I don't have to look at the actual data to know that the probability of having a boy (or not a girl) is 100% minus 49%, or 51%. Often, we state only one probability and leave the other unstated, as when we say that there is a 60% chance of rain tomorrow. Of course, that means there is a 40% chance that it will not rain.

> Be specific and careful about what you want to know when working with probabilities: if you ask the wrong question, you will get the wrong answer.

If there are multiple possible outcomes, things get a little more complicated, and we need to be clear about which outcome we are examining. For example, usually one thinks of only two main employee categories in local government: full time and part time. But any good HR manager knows that there are multiple categories. Usually a government would have four different categories: permanent full-time, permanent part-time, temporary full-time, and temporary part-time employees. If I pick an employee at random, there is a probability associated with each category. Added up, the probabilities of all the categories equal 100%:

Probability (permanent full time) + Probability (permanent part time) + Probability (temporary full time) + Probability (temporary part time) = 100%.

If we want to pick an employee at random and want to know the chance of getting a particular type of employee, we take the number of employees in that category divided by the number of total employees. If we know the probability of getting an employee in one category, we also know, automatically, the probability of *not* getting an employee in that category—in other words, the probability of getting an employee from one of all the other categories.

## Combining probabilities

What often confuses people is this kind of probability: the probability of not one characteristic, but of two or more characteristics that can be combined in different ways. If I am a firefighter, do I work night shifts or day shifts? Do I work weekends, weekdays, or both? Do I work full time or part time? Do I serve as a volunteer or professional staff? Do I have certification to deal with hazardous materials or not? Given the possible combinations, if may seem daunting to try to figure out the probability of a randomly selected firefighter being an uncertified volunteer working only night shifts on weekends. But when you break it down into parts, it is not so hard.

In the probability tree shown in the figure, we have two different characteristics: (1) whether someone is permanent or temporary (employee type), and (2) whether he or she is a full-time or a part-time employee (employee status). This gives us a set of options for each of the two characteristics, or four different kinds of outcomes, as you can see in Figure 5–1. Each set of options is considered an event.

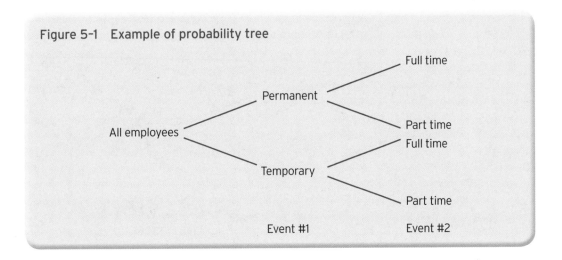

Figure 5-1   Example of probability tree

Let's fill out this probability tree to demonstrate how researchers use probabilities. Say that a local government has 100 employees, 70 of whom are permanent and 30 of whom are temporary. Our chart would look like the probability tree in Figure 5–2.

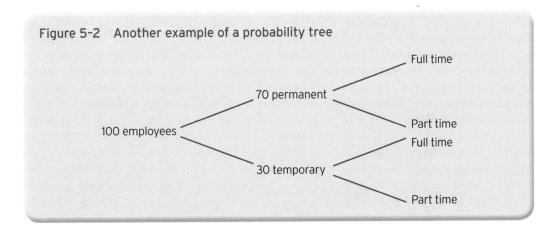

Figure 5-2   Another example of a probability tree

If you picked an employee at random, there is a 70% chance (70/100 or 0.70) that the employee would be permanent. Likewise, there is a 30% chance (30/100 or 0.30) that the employee would be temporary. Now let's add the next event: whether the employees are full time or part time. Of all the permanent employees, 50 work full time and 20 work part time. Of all the temporary employees, 5 are full time and 25 are part time. Let's put those numbers in (see Figure 5–3).

From the numbers in Figure 5–3, I can calculate a whole variety of probabilities. The key to doing this correctly is to understand exactly what you are measuring;

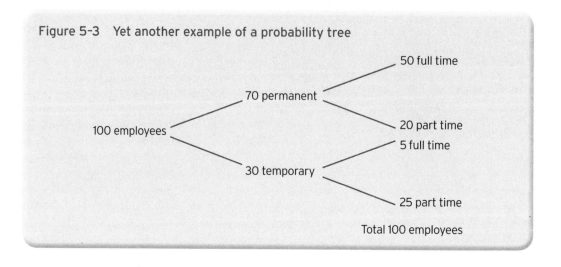

Figure 5-3    Yet another example of a probability tree

In other words, what is the likelihood of a particular outcome happening? What is it that you want to know? Figure 5–4 shows the tree with probabilities put in for each of the second events in addition to numbers. In each case, we are taking that individual part over the whole or, in other words, the specific "outcome" over all possible outcomes in that part of the tree.

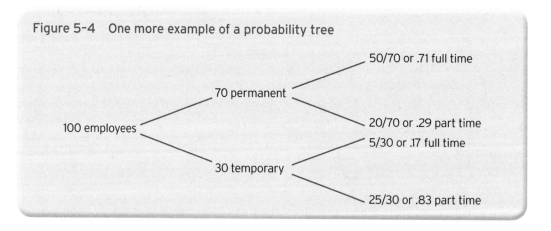

Figure 5-4    One more example of a probability tree

Of all the permanent employees, 71% are full time and 29% are part time. Of all the temporary employees, 17% are full time and 83% are part time. These are examples of **conditional probability;** that is, the probability is an outcome in the second event, given a particular outcome in the first event. In other words, we might say, "Given that an employee is permanent, there is about a 70% chance that he or she would be full time," or "Most permanent employees are full time." NOTICE! In this case, I said, "Given that an employee is permanent. . . ." This is not the full group of employees. We are only considering permanent employees. Permanent employees are our base for this ratio. For these probabilities, we are only on the top half of the tree, having followed the path up to permanent employees and, from there, calculated new probabilities for the next event or branch of the tree. How would you describe the probabilities in the bottom half?

***Probability of two or more events.***     Now, what if I want to know the probability of both events at the same time? That is, out of all the employees, what is the likelihood that I would meet someone who is both permanent *and* full time? NOTICE! In this case, I said "out of *all* the employees." It is the full group of employees. We are considering all employees. All employees are our base for this ratio. But for this, I would need to know the number of people in this specific joint category: the "joining" of permanent and full time. To find this out, we take the numbers that we show in Figure 5–4 and calculate the probabilities for each end point, which we now display in Figure 5–5.

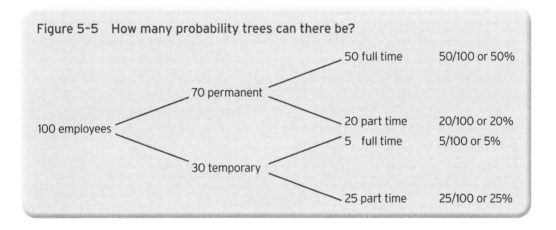

**Figure 5-5    How many probability trees can there be?**

I am using primarily local government work examples in this chapter, but understanding how probabilities work is necessary throughout our day-to-day life. When I was pestering my husband about having just one more baby, I went to the doctor and wanted to know what the likelihood was that we would have a healthy baby when I was 41 years old. She gave me many different numbers on lots of different aspects of pregnancy: conception, miscarriage, various genetic problems. She gave me probabilities of this, and probabilities of that, and I finally stopped her, and said, "What is the probability of me having a healthy baby at age 41?" She didn't know how to combine the probabilities.

I drew a tree and showed her that it was just a matter of the three events (probability of conception, probability of not having a miscarriage, and probability of not having any genetic problems). I wanted to know the probability of the path that led to only one particular outcome: a healthy baby. So, I multiplied the probability of conceiving at age 40, times the probability of not having a miscarriage at age 40, times the probability of the baby being healthy when the mom is 40. The result: 2.7%. The probability of not having a healthy baby (all other options): 97.3%. That put the whole issue into perspective.

However, remember how much I emphasized before that anything can happen, that there is no absolute certainty of any particular outcome? I am thrilled to report that my fourth child, Leo, was born healthy and happy about nine months later. *Anything* can happen.

***Joint probabilities.***    It is easy to calculate the **joint probabilities,** the probability of two things happening (such as being full time and being a permanent employee) when you know the final numbers. But what if you only have the probabilities with each event? For example, let's assume that the employee structure in another town is completely different. You don't have the numbers, but here is the information that the HR director sent you in an e-mail:

We are a beach resort town, so we have a lot more temporary employees than other towns. They make up 80% of our workforce. Of the temporary employees, to keep benefit costs down, about 95% are part time. We don't have any permanent part-time employees. We had to get rid of them in the last round of state budget cuts.

From this information, we can figure out the other percentages for our tree. If 80% of the employees are temporary, then the other 20% must be permanent. If there are no permanent part timers, then 100% of the permanent employees must be full time. And if 95% of the temporary employees are part time, then 5% of the temporary employees must be full time (see Figure 5–6).

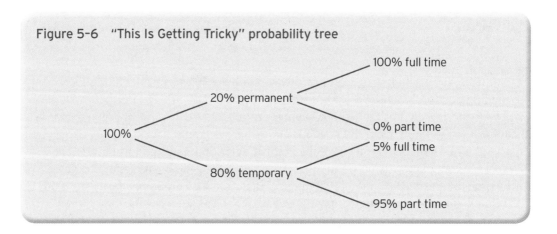

Figure 5-6    "This Is Getting Tricky" probability tree

100% full time

20% permanent

100%

0% part time

5% full time

80% temporary

95% part time

Now we can determine the joint probabilities by multiplying the probabilities in each branch of the tree.

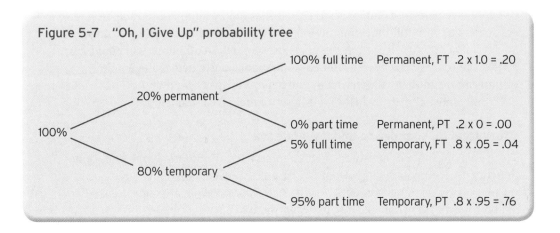

Figure 5-7    "Oh, I Give Up" probability tree

Just as with the number trees in Figures 5–4 and 5–5, the probabilities total 100%. Another way to present this same information is in a chart or table; using the information from that e-mail the HR director sent you, we can fill in the numbers (see Table 5–1). I just used 100 employees as an example because it matches 100%. But you could follow the information for any number of employees.

Table 5-1    Example of probability chart (thank goodness it's not a tree) using employee type information

| | Employee status | | |
|---|---|---|---|
| Employee type | Full time | Part time | Total |
| Permanent | 20 | 0 | 20 |
| Temporary | 4 | 76 | 80 |
| Total | 24 | 76 | 100 |

From a table like this, you can produce a wide array of probabilities as long as you keep straight what is the base (denominator) of the fraction and what is the portion (numerator) of the fraction; in other words, what particular outcome you are interested in over what group of outcomes. Take the following example of a simple problem that you can solve by using the numbers in Table 5–1:

You are planning the annual employee picnic and want to play a softball game pitting the permanent full-time players against the temporary part-time players. How many people would be available to serve as umpires? Four, just enough. I got the answer by adding the number of permanent full-time employees (20) to the number of temporary part-time employees (76). This would be compared to the other two entries, temporary full-time employees (4) and permanent part-time employees (0). You could get this answer from the chart or tree, too. In addition, you could also switch the order of the events. You could first consider whether the employee is full or part time, and then whether he or she is permanent or temporary. The result for each outcome is the same, just in a different order. Try it and see.

### Statistical independence and dependence

This is a good time to introduce the idea of **statistical independence and dependence.** The distinction is important because if two events are independent, there *is no* support for a connection between the two. If two events are dependent, there *is* support for a connection existing between the two.

Statistical independence exists when the probability of the first event equals the probability of the second event given the first event. In logic symbols, you would see this formula:

$p(A)$ = $p(A$ given $B)$, or the probability of A equals the probability of A given B.

Huh? In simpler terms, two events are independent if they are not related. Thus, assuming that they are not related, if one occurs, there is no change in the probability of the other event occurring. Knowing the probability of one event does not tell you anything about the probability of the other. Knowing someone is female does not tell you anything about what type of cell phone she is using. Knowing a house is in the "swank" neighborhood does not tell you if the occupants have a ping-pong table. (At least, I don't think it does.)

> Complex outcomes can be broken down into a simple series
> of individual events. Don't let complexity freak you out.

Let me give you a more realistic example: I am interviewing candidates for a summer internship and want to hire someone local. My assistant has told me that about half the candidates grew up in the immediate area (probability of being a "local" = 50%). The first candidate is ready to come in. My assistant says, "I think you will like her; she has lots of experience."

Now, does knowing that the person has experience tell you anything about whether that person is a local? Are these two things linked? Does the probability of being a local have any influence on being experienced? To put it in the format of our formula: does the probability of a person being experienced equal the probability of that person being experienced *given that* he or she is a local?

$p$(a person being experienced) = ? (a person being experienced) given *that* (a person is local).

I would say no. I would generally say that being a local and being experienced are not linked. They are independent. In other words, I think the probability of being a local is 50%. The probability of being a local, given that one is experienced, is still 50%. Knowing whether someone is experienced does not help me guess whether the person is a local.

## Probabilities not independent

Let's run through an example of two probabilities that are *not* independent. Using our previous example of full-time and part-time employees, if I know that the person standing in front of me is full time, would it help me to guess whether he or she is a permanent employee? Let's look at the formula:

Probability (permanent employee) = ? Probability (permanent employee given full time).

From Table 5–1 we know that there are 20 permanent employees out of all 100 employees. This means that the probability of being a permanent employee is 20%. That is the first part of our formula. For the second part of the formula, we need the number of permanent employees out of all full-time employees. The number of all full-time employees is 24. Of those, 20 are permanent. Thus, the probability of being permanent, given that the employee is full time, is 20 over 24, or 83%. Does 20% equal 83%? No! In this case, knowing that someone is full time *does* change the probability that the person is permanent, so we *can* use the information of full-time status to help with our guess about being permanent. The two probabilities—that of being full time and that of being permanent—are not independent. They are dependent.

## Combinations of attributes

Another way to see how two events can be dependent is by looking for certain combinations of attributes. For example, to continue with the same example, let's say you need to select a committee of employees. You choose the first person at random from all employees. What is the likelihood (probability) that the person is a permanent employee? As I said, it is 20%. What is the likelihood that the second person chosen is a permanent employee? You might guess 20% again, and you would be almost right. But the ratio is a little different. Instead of having 20 permanent employees to choose from, there are only 19: remember that we already chose one, so that person is out of the mix now! She is the first member of the committee. In addition, our total pool now consists of only 99 employees, instead of 100. So the probability of having a permanent employee is now 19 over 99, or 19%; that's close, but different.

When you have a very, very large pool of possible outcomes, a slight change such as pulling one person out doesn't show up in a difference in probabilities. But when the pool is small, the outcome of the first event (such as picking someone for a committee) does have an impact on the second event. Knowing who is chosen first affects my guess for who is chosen second. In the trees shown in the figures in this chapter, events are *dependent*, meaning that probabilities for the second event depend on what path you take in the first event. For *independent* events, probabilities for the second event do not depend on what path you take for the first event; they are the same whether you take the top path, bottom path, or any path for the first event.

Why is the distinction of dependence and independence important? It is a clue about association, which we will discuss in later chapters. If probabilities are dependent, then there is probably going to be an association between the two things, perhaps even a causal relationship. But we're getting ahead of ourselves. . . .

## "Hell, Chuck, the death in Red Oak just proves my point. We shouldn't rely

on volunteer firefighters to fight fires. They are more likely to die in those buildings." Rex and Will had joined Chuck at the bar after their golf game. Rex ran the local hobby shop, complete with model airplanes, buckets of clay, balsa wood, trading cards, and, recently, LEGO® sets. For some reason, LEGO® was the hot new hobby/toy, and he was selling LEGO® sets as fast as he could stock them. Wherever Rex was, Will could be found close behind. Will teased Rex about turning his childhood into his job, but he never seemed to be far from Rex's shop—or from the LEGO® sets.

The topic of conversation wasn't as light as the usual joking. Rex's father was a prominent community member and a strong advocate for increasing the professional firefighter force. Rex had become convinced that this was the right choice to make and was pressing his point with Chuck.

"I don't know, Rex. I just don't know what to do. Everyone at the meeting on Monday is going to focus on whether adding more volunteers to the fire squad is a good idea. Instead of us looking at the facts and trying to make the best decision, it is going to be very emotional," said Chuck. "I just don't want to get carried away with a lot of assumptions and make a bad decision."

"Well, you know what they say about assumptions: they make an ass out of you and. . . ," started Will, before Rex threw a pretzel at him. "Seriously, why not get the numbers before the meeting?"

"What do you mean?"

"Instead of letting people just assume volunteers are more at risk in fires, why not find out some facts. If a firefighter dies fighting a fire, is she or he more likely to be a volunteer or a professional?"

"It has got to be volunteer. C'mon, Will, don't you think the professionals know better what they are doing?"

"I'm not saying anything about anybody. I just want to know what the numbers actually are!"

Chuck just sat and chewed on his pretzel. "I have to stop by the office for a sec before we go get pizza, guys. See you at the Pizza Palace in about forty-five minutes? We may as well order a pitcher of pop this time instead of individual glasses, as long as we're all ordering Diet Coke."

Rex looked down at his no-longer-slim-and-trim belly. "Yeah, I guess so."

## Review questions

1. How would you explain probability to a kindergarten student?

2. How does the concept of *confidence* fit into a discussion of statistics?

3. What is an event? Give an example.

4. What is an outcome? Give an example.

5. What is the first rule of probability? Give an example.

6. What is a probability tree? Make a tree with 100 employees. You know that 65 are permanent and of those, 30 are full time. You also know that there are 50 full-time employees overall.

7. What are conditional probabilities? From the example in #6, what would be the conditional probabilities?

8. Make a probability tree or chart based on your own clothes. Assume you have 100 articles of clothing. What is the percentage of your clothes that are in dark colors? What percentage is for warm weather? What percentage of the dark is also for warm weather? What percentage of the lighter colored clothes is also for colder weather? Can you tell anything about your clothing choices with the resulting tree or table?

9. Create another probability tree using some data from your or a friend's workplace.

10. Use that probability tree to create a table. Write a brief paragraph stating if there seems to be a pattern in the resulting data or percentages, or not.

# That Picture Doesn't Look a Thing Like Me!

## 6

## [SAMPLES VERSUS POPULATIONS]

**Chuck sat down with his buddies.** The pitcher of Diet Coke was already half gone. But Chuck knew he had timed it just right: there was no pizza yet, but it must be on its way any minute. "Okay, guys, I set our new analyst on this, and she was able to find me the numbers in about two minutes, as usual."

"What do you mean?" asked Rex.

"You always show up right when the pizza is coming to the table. How do you do that?" joked Will. The waitperson placed the supreme pizza (minus olives) on the table and distributed the plates and napkins. "Anyone need forks?"

The three guys shook their heads no.

"Nina was able to get the numbers to answer whether a volunteer firefighter is more likely than a professional firefighter to die in the course of fighting a fire."

"Well, thanks for lightening up the conversation, Chuck!" said Rex.

"Come on, guys. You know that I am going to be grilled on this tomorrow night at the council meeting. So I better figure it out now. Look at this table." He placed a copy of the table (shown on the next page) before each of the men.

"Nationwide, out of the 85 firefighter deaths in 2008, volunteers did account for a higher percentage. But here's what is really interesting. Of all the professionals' deaths, almost half occurred at the fire ground; of all the volunteer deaths, however, only 21% occurred at the fire ground while almost half occurred while the volunteers were re- sponding to or returning from an alarm!" Chuck pointed at the numbers for emphasis.

"So if you are a volunteer, you're about twice as likely to die in a car crash on the way to the fire as to die at the fire?" Rex was very interested in the numbers, drawing his copy closer in.

Table 6-1   Comparison of on-duty deaths between career and volunteer firefighters, 2008

| Type of duty | Career firefighters | | Volunteer firefighters | |
|---|---|---|---|---|
| | No. | % | No. | % |
| Responding to or returning from alarm | 1 | 4 | 26 | 45 |
| Operating at fire ground | 12 | 44 | 12 | 21 |
| Operating at nonfire emergencies | 3 | 11 | 8 | 14 |
| Training | 2 | 7 | 5 | 9 |
| Other on-duty | 9 | 33 | 7 | 12 |
| Total | 27 | 100 | 58 | 100 |

Source: Reproduced with permission from Rita F. Fahy, Paul R. LeBlanc, and Joseph L. Molis, *Firefighter Fatalities in the United States–2008* (Quincy, Mass.: Fire Analysis and Research Division, National Fire Protection Association, copyright © 2009), 16.

Note: While 100 is shown for illustration purposes, actual percentages in the columns do not total 100% because of rounding.

"Yup," Chuck nodded.

"Wow. Volunteers are over ten times more likely to die going to or coming from the fire than professionals?"

"Yup."

"What are you guys talking about?" asked Will. His attention had been on the pizza.

"Look: 21% of volunteer deaths were at the fire ground, compared to 44% of professional firefighter deaths. That is where we get the 'about twice as likely' figure. And 45% of volunteer deaths were in car crashes (presumably, if they were traveling to or from the fire), but those accounted for only 4% of professional firefighter deaths. This 45% is 11 times higher than 4%. It's just a different way to say the same thing, but the comparisons are more impressive. Rex likes to be impressive," said Chuck with a smile. He reached for the biggest piece of pizza, wrapping the dripping, stretching cheese over the top as he pulled it off the pan.

"Okay, you have convinced me. Volunteers are not as likely to die in fighting a fire itself. So you can't use that argument to push for hiring only professionals. But you could use these numbers to argue that volunteers need some better way to get to a fire other than screaming down the road with just their regular car flashers going," said Will.

"What do our guys do, Chuck?" asked Rex. "Do they go straight to the fire, or do they report to the station and then use a fire station vehicle?"

"I'm not sure, but now I am really curious. I'm also curious about the location of our fires—you know, if they are more rural than in town, that kind of thing. Also, just because these are national figures doesn't mean they hold for us. We might have a much better safety record."

"Oh, yeah, Chuck, Stan, and his boys are real safe drivers!" Everyone laughed. Stan was a prominent volunteer firefighter and had the newest F150 pickup in town. He loved showing how much power it had, and if asked about safe drivers, Stan's name would not necessarily be the first to jump to mind.

Rex looked at the sheet. "Are these all the deaths, or just a sample?"

"Huh?" Chuck almost choked on his slice. "You're starting to talk like Nina!"

"It looks like these are all the deaths in 2008. It is a population. A sample is a smaller group, a subgroup you might say, that represents the larger population. But I don't think it matters; I think we are looking at the wrong thing. Wouldn't it be better to look at injuries? They would be a lot more common and might give you a different picture. Of course, it would be impossible to get a full population of injury data for the country. And like you said, national figures lump everything together: cities, counties, big, small. I might just look at some injury figures for similar-size towns in the Midwest—not all, though, because that would be too much work, even if you could get the data. Just a sample."

"Now I *know* you are talking like Nina!"


If you wanted to know what people thought about a presidential candidate before an election, it would be impossible to interview everyone in the country. You would have to interview just some of the people and hope these folks' views reflected general national opinion. This process—hoping the opinion or behavior of a subgroup is representative of the larger group—is called **sampling.**

Remember how, in Chapter 4, when working with standard deviations within a population, we knew that in normal curves, 68% of all observations fall within one standard deviation of the mean, 95% of all observations lie within two standard deviations of the mean, and 99.9% of all observations fall within three standard deviations of the mean? We use the same ratios with sample data but call them something different: sample error. With a population, we use standard deviations and the mean or average to get a sense of what the overall data picture is like. With samples, we work with the sample mean and sample errors.

In the following sections I'll talk about where the idea of sample error comes from and how it is used. But it will be helpful through the discussion to keep in the back of your head what the normal curve looks like: an average in the middle, and brackets for one, two, or three standard deviations OR sample errors above and below the mean.

## Good samples and good estimates

Almost all research is based on samples. Samples allow us to take a small number of observations and make inferences about the larger population. Samples give us estimates. If we are interested in how poor a community is, we might use a sample of household incomes to get an estimate. If we want to know how experienced a police force is, we might use a sample of officers' years on the job to get an estimate. Whatever it is we want to know, samples give us an estimate of the "true" or "real" or exact value, the value we would get if we could gather information from the entire population.

If we wanted to know the "true" level of poverty in a community, we would have to know everyone's household income. If we wanted to know the "true" level of experience for the whole police force, we would need to know how many years every single officer has served. A final example: say that a local government wants to know the citizens' opinions about building a new public swimming pool on the east side of town. The government could hire a consulting firm to telephone everyone in town, but, of course, that is much too expensive and practically impossible.

Therefore, instead of knowing the *true* average opinion by talking to everyone in town, the local government has to rely instead on an *estimate* of the true average opinion, by taking a sample.

Any estimate is going to include some *error* (it is hard to imagine getting an estimate that is exactly the same as the value we would get if we were able to get all the data from the whole population), so how do we know if our estimate is a good one? This is really the question people ask when they say "Is it a good sample?" A good sample should result in a good estimate most of the time. But no matter how hard we try, we will always have some error in our sample. How do we get a sense of how much error there is?

## Sample error

Analysts do this with a number called the **sample error.** The sample error is the estimate of how much error we have in our sample.

The formula for sampling error, or sample error, is

$$\text{Sample error} = \frac{\text{Standard deviation for sampling population}}{\text{Square root of sample size}}.$$

Don't worry too much about the formula because, as with standard deviation, most spreadsheet programs will calculate it for you. For those of you who are data nerds, *sample error* is the same as *standard error,* a statistical term used in a slightly different context. I will be using only *sample error,* to be consistent.

### Size of sample error is related to the spread, or dispersion, of the distribution of the sample data

In Chapter 4, we showed how we can assume that any data distribution is shaped like a normal curve. We also discussed how standard deviation helped us measure if the distribution (and the associated normal curve), was narrow and tightly distributed or spread out and widely distributed. As you can see from the formula, if the standard deviation for the population is large compared to the population mean (the normal curve is spread out), the sample error will be too. Is there a lot of variation in our sample data, with a wide distribution, as shown in Figure 6–1, or less variation, with a narrow distribution, as shown in Figure 6–2? If our curve looks like Figure 6–1, our sample has a lot of error.

**Figure 6-1   Sample with lots of variation (and thus lots of error)**

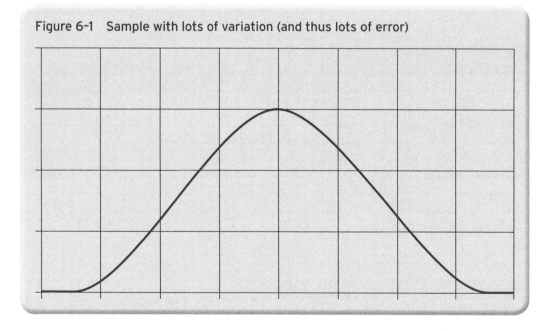

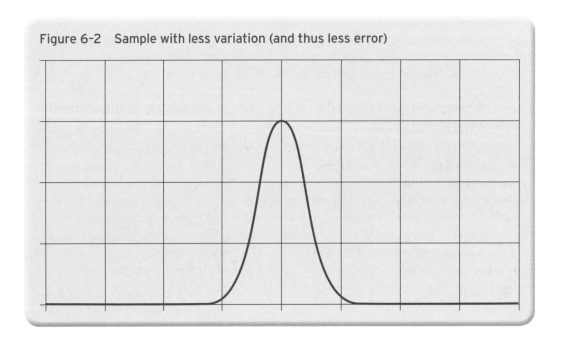

Figure 6-2   Sample with less variation (and thus less error)

## Confidence interval

Now, do you remember when we looked at a population with a normal distribution in Chapter 4? We found out what the standard deviation was and used the *z*-score to tell us what percentage of values fell between two numbers, or what percentage of the values in the population was above or below any particular number. In the same way, we can use the sample error to give us a range within which we hope the true mean falls. This range, which is on either side of the sample mean, is called the **con-fidence interval**. We usually believe that the **true mean** falls somewhere within this range. In Figure 6–3, the sample average or mean is 50, but the confidence interval is +/– 3. In other words, while our estimate of the average is 50, we are saying that we hope and expect the true mean to really be somewhere between 47 and 53.

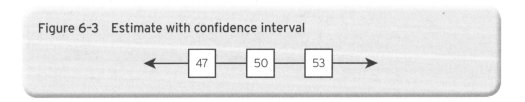

Figure 6-3   Estimate with confidence interval

How do we determine this range? I want to repeat something I talked about at the beginning of the chapter. When working with populations and standard deviations, we knew that in normal curves, 68% of all observations fall within one standard deviation of the mean, 95% of all observations lie within two standard deviations of the mean, and 99.9% of all observations fall within three standard deviations of the mean.

The same ratios work with sample error. Just as we used standard deviations as a measuring stick with population data and called it a $z$-score, we can use sample error as a measuring stick with a sample and call it a **t-score.** $Z$-score and $t$-score are the same concept. With a sample of over 30 observations (not a number chosen at random, as you'll see shortly!), 95% of those observations will fall between two sample errors above and two sample errors below the mean.

> What you want to find is the "true mean," the real average if we were able to use all the data from a population. A sample mean is an estimate of the true mean. And estimates are almost always off.

If we want a 95% confidence interval, we would figure out our sample mean and count two sample errors above and below it. Two sample errors above and below the mean is the same as a $t$-score of $+/- 2$. The $t$-score is the number of sample errors a point is away from the mean in the sample.

### Confidence intervals and margin of error

The confidence interval is commonly called the margin of error. With samples, we are not sure if the mean in any one sample is close to the "true or real mean." If we put "brackets" around our sample mean—including a lower value and a higher value—we give ourselves a **margin of error** for our estimate. We give our audience a sense of the range around the sample mean in which the true mean could fall; in other words, how precise are we in our estimate? We use sample errors to make these brackets.

- If we use wide brackets, so wide that we are 99.9% sure that the true mean falls inside the brackets, our margin of error would be three sample errors above and below the mean.

- Most researchers use brackets that are two sample errors above and below the mean, being 95% confident the true mean falls somewhere between the brackets, or somewhere within the margin of error.

- If we use tight brackets, only one sample error above and below the mean, we would be only 68% confident the true mean would fall inside the brackets.

"Brackets" is not a very statistics-like term, so instead, statisticians use the term that I introduced earlier: confidence interval. Brackets, margin of error, confidence intervals—all the same thing, used in different contexts.

### T-score

The sample error is useful in the third way. In Chapter 4, we could consider any point from a population and know how far away it was from that population's mean by measuring the distance in terms of standard deviations. This allowed us to understand whether the observation in front of us was dramatically different from the rest of the data. If an observation was more than two standard deviations above or below the mean (as measured by its $z$-score), it was located in the tails of the distribution of the population; it was a data point very different from the average.

The same logic goes for samples, but instead of using standard deviations and $z$-scores, we use sample errors and $t$-scores. The formula for a $t$-score is

$$\frac{\text{Sample mean} - \text{the population mean}}{\text{Standard error}} .$$

What this formula says is that if the sample mean is far away from the true mean of the population, the sample is different from the population.

Now sometimes we don't know the true mean; we just have a comparison point that we use as a reference mean—for example, the mean from the population of data from last year, or the mean from the population of data from another local government, or what we *think* the true mean is. The mechanics are the same whether we use the true mean or the reference mean from a comparison population.

We are measuring the distance between two points: the sample mean and the reference mean. And our measuring stick is the sample error for our sample.

> With populations, you use standard deviations and $z$-scores.
> With samples, you use sample errors and $t$-scores.

Here's an example: Let's say that in the middle of the fiscal year, the county manager wants to know if the gas bill for the whole fiscal year for the fire department vehicles will be higher this year. The average weekly gas bill for last year was $750. The manager asks you to take a sample of weeks from the current fiscal year so she can estimate this year's weekly average. You take the sample. You calculate the average weekly bill. It is $830. You calculate the sample error. It is $15. What can you tell the manager?

"Ms. Gomez, if the pattern holds and gas prices don't change much, it looks like we are going to have an average weekly gas bill of $830, give or take $30."

"What do you mean, give or take, Leo?"

"I mean that this is just an estimate. At the end of the year, the true average probably won't be exactly $830. I'm very confident," Leo pauses, "actually 95% confident that at the end of the year it shouldn't be less than $800 or more than $860."

Leo did a quick calculation in his head to reassure himself that he had given the manager the right brackets. Math was not his thing. He had subtracted two sample errors from the sample mean to get the low end of the bracket, and added two sample errors to get the high end. Since the sample error was $15, he doubled it, and that means $30 below and $30 above. Okay, he's safe.

## Sample size

This is where the sample size is important. Remember how we discussed that most data populations we encounter either will have a normal distribution, more or less, or can be assumed to have a normal distribution (via the central limit theorem, remember)? That is also true in samples above 30 observations. Up to 30, the curve is not exactly normal; it tends to be flatter. The percentages we commonly use at one, two, or three standard deviations away from the mean (68%, 95%, and 99%) are different for $z$-scores in samples below 30 observations.

In other words, under 30, $t$-scores are slightly different from $z$-scores. Above 30, $z$-scores and $t$-scores mirror each other exactly in terms of the percentage under the curve between any two points. If your sample is under 30, the computer will make the appropriate adjustment to the values for the confidence interval, so the constraint of 30 observations is not that meaningful. However, most analysts working with samples want to have a much larger sample size anyway, just like pixels on a television screen. The more points used, the clearer the picture. For statistics, the more observations used, the clearer the patterns.

Most textbooks on statistics will include a full $z$-score table and a full $t$-score table, showing the percentage under the curve for each value of a $z$-score or $t$-score. I don't present these tables here because most data analysis programs will do the calculation for you. But you should recognize that with a *population* of data, the placement of any point in the distribution can be measured in standard deviations and $z$-scores; with a *sample* of data, the placement of any point in the distribution can be measured in sample errors and $t$-scores.

## Comparing two samples

*T*-scores are also used to understand if two samples are similar or different.

Let's say there is a legislative proposal in a western state to cut administrative costs across the board for all fire districts. The state budget is in the red to the tune of three billion dollars, and everyone is going to feel some pain.

"It costs about the same to oversee one fire district as another, right? So cut them all the same amount of dollars; that is fair, I think," states a legislator in favor of the measure.

But another legislator, from the mountainous area in the northwestern part of the state, thinks the costs in her fire district are a lot lower, so an across-the-board dollar cut would really hurt.

"I am not so sure the costs are the same. Let's take a sample of some of the districts in my neck of the woods and compare it to a sample from the districts down by you. Let's see if there is a big difference in average administrative costs. My little sister is in Western State's MPA program, and she can get the data for us."

***From the same population, or not.***    In statistical terms, we want to compare two samples and ask, Are they really from the same population? Or, do they represent two distinct groups? In this case, we are taking samples of administrative costs from two different parts of the state. If administrative costs are generally the same everywhere, the samples will have means that are not that far from each other, and we can say the samples come from the same population. However, if administrative costs actually do differ by region, the sample means are likely to be farther apart, and we would say that the second legislator is correct: using the same dollar cut would be unfair because some districts have higher or lower total costs than others do. In other words, the two areas should be considered as two different populations, and we have a sample from each. We do not have two samples from the same population.

If you put the samples on the same graph, it would it look like Figure 6–4:

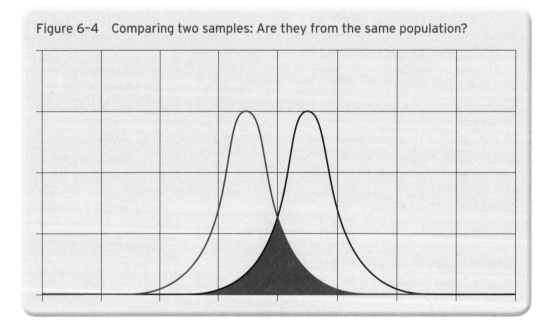

Figure 6-4    Comparing two samples: Are they from the same population?

Or like Figure 6–5:

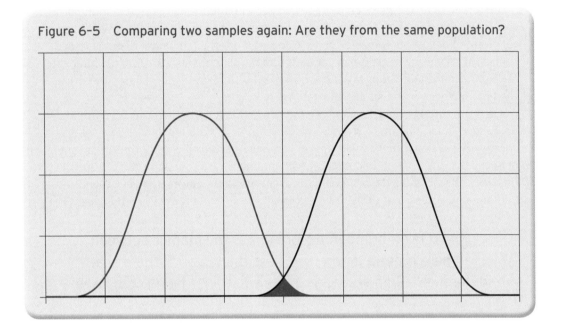

Figure 6-5    Comparing two samples again: Are they from the same population?

The math is slightly different here because instead of one sample error from one sample, we have two sample errors from two samples. In this case, the computer will calculate an average sample error from each sample.[1] Once we have the mean and sample error for each sample, we return to the idea that we are going to measure the distance between two points. In this case, with two samples, we want to measure the distance between the two sample means using a formula that combines the sample errors from each. As *t*-scores, this combination of sample errors gives us the same measuring stick that we use when comparing a sample mean with a true mean. If the distance is above 1.96, or more than around two sample errors (*t*-score = 1.96, or 2), we are 95% confident that the two samples are from two different populations. If the distance is not that great—say, under one sample error—we can't confidently say that

---

1  Your software program may ask you what type of "variance" you are assuming exists in the samples. The variance is the average squared deviation of each number in the sample from the mean. When we want to measure the dispersion in our data, the variance is the value of which we take the square root to get the standard deviation. Or, in other words, if you squared the standard deviation, you would have the variance. It is used far less than standard deviation in statistics, which is why we do not go into it much here. Always assume that the samples have unequal variances. This is the highest standard to meet with tests of statistical significance. If the difference is statistically significant between two groups with unequal variances, it will be statistically significant in all other cases. This way, you don't have to worry about whether your assumption is correct; you just automatically choose the toughest standard to beat.

the two samples are from different populations. We have to conclude that the two samples are from the same population, and any difference in the means is random.

Let's stop here and go back to the example. The little sister gathered administrative costs from the two samples. She calculated the *t*-score. It was 0.8. Which legislator won the debate? If you said the first one, you are right. The fire districts ended up having to cut the same dollar amount of administrative costs. (It made almost no difference to the state budget deficit, however. Administrative costs are not where the big money is in almost any budget.)

Let's run through another example. Let's say that a department has instituted a new scheduling program to reduce overtime hours. It's a large department, like a social services department in an urban area, such as the New York City Department of Social Services, which had over 15,000 employees at the time of the writing of this book. Because the department records are not fully automated yet, it would be too time-consuming and difficult to gather all the HR data for every employee.

## The rule of thumb: A *t*-score of 2 is the marker between "there is not a difference" (less than 2) and "there *is* a difference" (2 and greater) in the two things being compared.

Instead, it is much more reasonable to take a sample of employees—say, one thousand—and look at the average number of overtime hours per person. To what would we compare it? To know if the new scheduling program is reducing hours, we need to compare data from the new program to something else. Luckily, we do have all the information for all employees from the previous year! So we are comparing a sample from this year to a population from last year. Here are the main descriptive statistics from our sample, already calculated for you by your extremely capable MPA summer intern:

Sample mean (mean from the sample under the current, new program): 7.5
Population mean (taken from previous research: mean from all of last year,
    before the new scheduling program took effect): 6.5
Sample error: 0.5
(7.5 − 6.5) / 0.5 = 2.0
The *t*-score is 2. What can we say?

You would be correct if you answered, "Of course, as soon as I saw the *t*-score was 2, I knew the new program was making a difference. Having a *t*-score of 2 meant that there was a meaningful, real distance between the average overtime hours per person from last year and the average overtime hours per person under the new program."

### Second use of "confidence"

We've talked briefly about the confidence interval: the two values above and below our sample mean between which we hope the true mean falls. Now we need to understand confidence intervals at a deeper level and learn a different use of the word *confidence:* **confidence level.**

### Returning to the concept of a confidence interval

First, let's review the basic idea behind a confidence *interval*. With a sample, we usually want to know how close our sample mean is to the true mean. So, we use a confidence interval, or margin of error, around the sample mean. We think the true mean will fall between those brackets. The confidence interval is the range between the lower bracket value and the higher bracket value. Sometimes people just say "plus or minus *x*-number of percentage points" instead of giving the actual numbers. For example, opinion polls might report, "public approval of Congress is at an all-time low, only 15%." If you read the fine print about how they got this number, it would be from a random sample, and there would be a margin of error reported. Often with opinion polls, this is "plus or minus three percentage points." This means that if we could poll everyone in the United States, the true percentage of people approving of Congress could be as low as 12% or as high as 18%. The confidence interval is 12% to 18%.

Where would the poller get the value of three percentage points? Well, first the poller would have to think ahead. How confident does he want to be when he gives a value to the newspaper? Hmmm. If he is an easygoing guy and doesn't care too much if the estimate is correct—that is, he just wants to get a general range of where public opinion is—he might say that being 90% confident is enough. In that case, he would use a confidence interval that is one sample error below and above the sample mean, because 90% confidence means using brackets of one sample error below and above the sample mean. In this example, the sample error is 1.5 percentage points. His brackets would have been tighter than the poll's brackets, for a confidence interval of 13.5% to 16.5%.

If he is a middle-of-the-road guy, one wanting to use the industry standard for his estimate, he would want to be 95% confident. The industry standard of 95% confident is associated with two sample errors below and above the sample mean. Two sample errors in our example equal 3 percentage points. The middle-of-the-road person would say he was 95% confident that the true public approval rating for Congress was somewhere between 12% and 18% (sound familiar?).

If he is nervous and wants to be very, very confident—say 99.9% confident—that the true measure of congressional approval fell inside the brackets, he would use three sample errors around the sample mean. He could be 99.9% confident in reporting the congressional approval was somewhere between a 10.5% and 19.5% confidence interval.

### Confidence level

These examples connect confidence intervals with the researcher's chosen confidence level. But more often, we leave the intervals behind and focus just on our confidence level.

Like confidence intervals, confidence levels have to do with how good our sample is. With confidence levels, though, we focus on our conclusion: how confident are we when we draw a conclusion from our data? In the example of average overtime hours per person, how confident would the intern be in reporting that the new program was making a difference? A confidence level is similar to the idea behind a confidence interval, but we use it in a different way.

Confidence is a sense of surety, a sense of being right, of doing something well. In statistics, however, *confidence* has a very specific meaning, and it relates to the idea of *probabilities*. If you wanted to know the average income for the city of Seattle and could interview everyone in the city, you would be able to calculate the *exact* average income. Because it is a population, you would be *certain* about the average income you calculate. There is no chance that you could be wrong, absent human error in recording the data or in doing the math.

However, in a survey, for example, there is always a chance that our sample, for some reason, does not accurately reflect average income in Seattle (and here we come back to the idea of sample error). Maybe Bill Gates randomly appeared in our sample and skewed the average to the right or, in other words, pushed the sample average up. Maybe our survey staff decided to interview only people in a very poor part of town, and as a result, the sample average is too low. Or maybe, just by chance (because remember that anything can be random), our survey staff only encountered "outliers" who didn't really reflect a representative sample of Seattle citizens.

### Probability of being wrong: *P* value

As we discussed in Chapter 5, with any sample we can never be 100% confident that our estimate perfectly matches reality. There is always the probability that our estimate is wrong. This probability of being "wrong" is called the **p value.** In other words, what is the chance that any pattern I see is just random noise? I don't want to shout some conclusion from the mountaintop if there is a good chance the conclusion is just due to a random pattern in the data. So, as analysts, we are left with deciding how confident we want to be in our conclusions. Analysts normally choose one of three levels of confidence:

- 90% confident. If you choose this confidence level, you are allowing yourself a 10% chance that the conclusions drawn from your data could be wrong. That is, you agree to the standard that one out of ten times, you might draw the wrong conclusion from the data. The 90% confidence level is associated with a *p* value of .10. (Makes sense, right? If you want to be 90% sure that you have the right answer, you accept a 10% chance of being wrong, thereby covering 100% of all possibilities.)

- 95% confident. If you choose this confidence level, you are allowing yourself a 5% chance that the conclusions drawn from your data could be wrong. That is, you agree to the standard that one out of twenty times, you might draw the wrong conclusion from the data. The probability of being wrong is only 5%, or a *p* value of .05.

- 99.9% confident. If you choose this confidence level, you are allowing yourself only a 0.1% chance that the conclusions drawn from your data could be wrong. That is, you agree to the standard that only one out of one thousand times, you might draw the wrong conclusion from the data. The probability of being wrong is only 0.1%, or a *p* value of .001.

These values—90%, 95%, 99.9%—are all common benchmarks. In a study, however, you might have a *p* value of .08. This means there is an 8% chance that any pattern in your data is just random. Or you might have a *p* value of .25, which means there is a 25% chance that the pattern you see is just random.

## Statistical significance

Researchers usually don't care about knowing the exact *p* value. You need to remember that all the results in a study using samples are estimates. So reporting the exact *p* value implies a precision that is not there. Instead, we use the 90%, 95%, and 99.9% benchmarks for confidence levels. This is where a very important term enters the picture: **statistical significance.** A result is **statistically significant** if the *p* value meets or is less than one of the three *p* value benchmarks. In practical terms, it means the patterns in the data are strong enough that they are *not* likely to have occurred by random chance. In the examples used in the previous paragraph, a *p* value of .08 meets the benchmark of being at least 90% confident the pattern you see in the data is not random. There is only an 8% chance the patterns could be random. For many researchers, this is an acceptable finding to make a decision based on the conclusions from the analysis. In contrast, a *p* value of .25 doesn't meet any of the benchmarks. There is a 25% chance any pattern in the data could be random. For most researchers this is too high of a chance to use these data in this analysis in making an important decision.

Now, you like to be right all the time, correct? So do I. But remember: I said that nothing is certain. With sample data, no matter how clear the pattern in the data, there is always a chance that the pattern is just random. Perhaps it is an infinitesimal chance, but it is still a chance. So there is always a chance that we could be wrong. A result is only as strong as its *p* value. If you are like me, and like to be right, you want to have results that meet the highest standards of confidence—that is, 99.9% confident, or a *p* value of .001.

- If you have a result associated with a *p* value of *.10 or below,* it is said to be **statistically significant** at the .10 level.

- If you have a result associated with a *p* value of *.05 or below,* it is said to be **statistically significant** at the .05 level.

- If you have a result associated with a *p* value of *.001 or below,* it is said to be **statistically significant** at the .001 level.
- If you have a result with a *p* value of .000 that means it is so low that only the zeros in the first three decimal places show up on the printout. You have extreme confidence in the results.

## Statistics are all about confidence!

Research with very high stakes (e.g., testing a vaccine for pandemic flu when up to 50% of the population may receive the medicine or testing an antibiotic for newborn babies when a mistake could mean death) may even warrant a 99.9% confidence level as a standard. That is, you want to be very, very certain of your conclusions, with a chance of only 1 out of 10,000 times that you will be wrong. In these cases, you want to allow a *p* value of only .0001, or a .01% chance of being wrong.

For every confidence level, from .01% to 54% to 99.9% and all points in between, there is an associated *p* value. And for every *p* value, there is an associated *t*-score. In Table 6-2, we bring confidence levels, *p* values, and *t*-scores together. To reach a higher confidence level, you must reach a lower *p* value (or less likelihood that you will reach a wrong conclusion). A lower *p* value happens when the *t*-score is higher. And a high *t*-score happens, if you remember, when there is a large difference between the two things you are comparing, as measured in sample errors (sample and population, two samples, etc.). This difference is measured in intervals by the *t*-score. The higher the *t*, the lower the *p*. The lower the *p*, the more confident you are that there is a difference between what you are comparing.

### Interpreting the findings

Table 6-2    Confidence levels and associated *p* values and *t*-scores.

| Confidence level, % | p value | t-score |
|---|---|---|
| 90 | .10 | 1.64 |
| 95 | .05 | 1.96 (or 2, as a rule of thumb) |
| 99 | .01 | 2.58 |

As a consumer of statistical information, I believe that none of the individual calculations is as important as understanding how to interpret the findings. Enter the beauty of computers, since they can do the work for you! Most of you will have someone else do your actual analysis, but you must be able to understand it and interpret it for the public or elected officials or department managers. For you, I hope this chapter prompts you to ask the following three questions when comparing two processes or practices:

1. Was there a difference?

2. Is that difference statistically significant?

3. How confident can you be in that conclusion?

## Hypothesis and null hypothesis

You might notice that I have not used the term *hypothesis* recently. That is because, outside of dissertations and class presentations (and notwithstanding our discussion in Chapter 1), most public administrators don't use that term. Officially, a hypothesis is a suggested explanation for an observable phenomenon or for a reasoned proposal predicting a possible causal correlation among multiple phenomena. Huh? I usually describe it as a guess, a guess that something is different from something else (and if it is, why? or if it is not, why not?) or that there is a relationship between two things.

The term *null hypothesis* denotes the opposite: that there is *not* a difference between two things, that there is no relationship between them, such that nothing is going on. The formal terms may be too technical for everyday use in government. That is why, in this book, I focus on the term *hypothesis* and its meaning in Chapter 1 and then for the rest of the chapters only on the idea of asking whether there is a difference between two things because that is how we actually use hypotheses every day in public administration. We have not been using the term, but inferential statistics is really about hypothesis testing. We ask, "Is there a difference? Is something going on?" (Is the hypothesis supported by the data?) Or, is there not really a difference? Is nothing going on? (Is the null hypothesis supported by the data?)

## Type I and Type II errors

You may encounter two other statistical terms related to confidence levels and statistical significance that are hard to remember and use every day, but whose meanings are important: **Type I** and **Type II errors.** As we've talked about in this chapter, when you draw a conclusion that is based on data, you have to decide on a level of confidence. How high is the evidence bar going to be before you accept a conclusion?

Many would argue that the bar should be as high as possible to ensure that we are drawing the correct conclusion. We all want to be right, right? However, when the bar is set very high, there is always a chance that we may fail to acknowledge a real difference or a real relationship. On the other hand, if we set the bar too low, there is a chance that we will jump to an incorrect conclusion. Damned if you do, and damned if you don't.

A Type I error occurs when you set the bar too low. A Type II error occurs when you set the bar too high. If you try to minimize Type I errors, you increase the chance that you will commit Type II errors. If you try to minimize Type II errors, you increase the chance that you will commit Type I errors. There is no appropriate confidence level to use for all questions. The standard you use—90%, 95%, or 99.9% confidence—should be appropriate for the question at hand, and of course, that is a subjective call.

## Material significance

There is one more very important question in statistics. We have discussed how statisticians use statistical significance, referring to whether or not we reach the confidence level we choose as our benchmark for making a conclusion based on the data. This means: Can we really say there is a difference? Is the *t*-score high enough (which is the same as saying, is the *p* value low enough? Remember the higher the *t*, the lower the *p*)? Can we say with confidence that there is a difference between two samples or groups? Can we say that there was a statistically significant change from last year to this year?

This brings us to the problem with statisticians: sometimes we focus so much on statistical significance that we miss the big picture. So, yes, we may be able to say with confidence that there is a difference, but *does that difference really matter?* This is called **material significance.**

> Can we say with confidence that there is a difference?
> This is called *statistical significance*. If so, does the difference
> really matter in any practical way? This is called *material
> significance*.

Statistical significance is important when you want to say whether there is a difference. Nevertheless, analysts must use their own judgment as to whether the difference is enough to make or change policy—that is, whether it has material significance. I can probably prove with some level of statistical significance that a change in a process, such as an accounting system, would save $100 over a year. The question is: is that a large enough amount of money to warrant making the change?

In some cases, you make decisions not based on data but based on politics, equity, compensation, the law, or community values. Don't waste time on the analysis described here if finding statistical significance will not have an impact on your decision—that is, if the decision is not really about the data at hand. And even if the decision depends on the data, be wary of analysis that describes only statistical significance. Be sure to include material significance in your considerations.

# The pizza was gone. The guys had splurged on a second pitcher of pop and got regular Coke. The Pizza Palace was slowing down, with only one large family still in the adjoining room. The kids were running around in the back poolroom, pretending to play the working and broken video games; the moms had run out of quarters at least a half hour ago.

"Thanks for the pizza, guys. See you next week," said Chuck.

"Not if we see you first!" replied Rex. Chuck expected that reply. It was the running joke of the last six months. He hoped the group would come up with a new one . . . soon.

"Hey, you almost forgot! Pitch in, buddy!" Will said. This was another of the guys' running jokes: to make a halfhearted effort to see if one of them could slip out without paying. It was a golden rule that each paid an equal share so that they never got into an argument over who would pick up the bill.

Outside, the evening had turned soft, with the sun just down but darkness still a little way off. The crickets and cicadas had started up in earnest, and the frogs in the ditches joined in. Otherwise, Council Top was quiet. There were not even any teenage cruisers out yet. It was hard to think about fires, firefighters, statistics, and death.

Coming up from behind, Rex broke into Chuck's thoughts. "Are you really going to try to get some data on the firefighter issue?"

"Yeah. I would really like to know if there is a difference between how volunteer and professional firefighters do. Not in terms of the quality of their work—I know they bust their butts all the time, and goodness knows they put in enough time—but I wonder if volunteers are injured more than professionals, and if so, whether we could do something about it. It just seems fair."

"Not to mention the insurance money the city would save?" Will said.

"Oh, of course. The better our record, the better the rates. But you know it's more than that," said Chuck.

"I know, I know," Rex said softly. "I feel bad for the folks in Red Oak, too. It is hard for a small town to lose a firefighter. You know, the council might not tell you, but folks think you are a great city manager, Chuck. Don't worry about it too much. See you at the course on Saturday. Same time. And if you want to see the new ripsaw I got, stop by the garage some day after work."

"See you!" said Will, walking across the gravel parking lot. The last family was finally leaving the Pizza Palace, and the lighted sign above the parking lot was now dark.

"Not if I see you first!" laughed Chuck.

## Review questions

1. What is a *t*-score and how does it differ from a *z*-score?

2. Describe the concept of a *confidence interval*. How would you use it with data?

3. If the distribution in our sample is small and narrow, what does this suggest about our sample error?

4. Define the *p* value and describe a circumstance in which it would be useful.

5. If our data have a *p* value of .05, what does this mean? What is our corresponding confidence level?

6. What is the difference between confidence intervals and confidence levels?

7. In a study with very high stakes, such as testing a new medication for use with cancer patients, what would you want your confidence level to be? Why? What would be your corresponding *t*-score and *p* value?

8. Write a sample hypothesis. Write the corresponding null hypothesis.

9. Define Type I and Type II errors, and explain how they affect research.

10. What is the difference between material significance and statistical significance? Is one more important than the other? Give an example of a situation where you might find statistical significance but not material significance.

## 7

# The Poll Numbers Are In, and in the Lead Is....

## [TAKING A SAMPLE]

**Chuck had asked the city council to put off the vote** on the firefighter position for two months. He argued that he wanted to reconsider staffing in the entire department–that the department had grown slowly over the years, with someone added full time here and someone else added part time there, but that no one had looked at the current structure for over a decade. "We don't know if the department is right for our city for the next ten years. This is an opportunity to take a step back and consider if we grew in the right way for our current needs. I hate to keep adding to the department incrementally. I want to be deliberative about what we do, in line with a department plan."

"Do you think we need a strategic plan for the department?" asked the chair. The public works department had taken on a strategic planning effort three years ago, and its success inside the department and its improved relationship with other departments had encouraged the council to ask about planning in other departments at any opportunity.

"No, maybe not a strategic plan," Chuck said slowly. "But more information about adding just one position. I would like to involve the firefighters more, and perhaps gather some comparison survey data from similar jurisdictions on injury rates for volunteer versus professional firefighters. If there is a difference, a material difference, I would like to know why and see if we can do anything to change it. I would also like to survey the firefighters, both volunteer and professional, about their satisfaction with their work."

Like all good local government managers, Chuck was careful about his public safety workers. The firefighters, police officers, and emergency medical service personnel were the most popular folks in town. They visited the school, hosted pancake breakfasts, and, once a year during the city's annual harvest festival, let the kids ride slowly around town on the fire engine with sirens blaring.

"Are you talking about a study for which we'd have to hire a consultant?" Council Member Maxwell was always careful about money, and she hated consultants.

"No, I think we can do a solid analysis with Nina. She has experience with these kinds of surveys and knows how to get a good sample."

"Will you get good enough information from a survey? Seems to me you want to talk to everyone, don't you? Would a sample really tell you what you want to know? Don't you need to talk to a whole bunch of people to get good information?" Maxwell was skeptical about everything. It was amazing she ever voted yes on any proposal. That was probably why she had been reelected so many times.

Nina stood up. "Actually, we can talk to a sample of the employees and get fairly solid results, Councilman Maxwell. But I will make sure that we apply the highest reasonable standards to the analysis so that we are very confident in our findings."

That sounded just professional enough to impress the council member without making her feel, well, dumb. Nina had already impressed her with an analysis of room occupancy taxes on the hotels in town. If Nina said that she could do it, Maxwell believed her.

"Well, I don't like waiting, but I agree that we could use more information. And I certainly believe that we should not add permanent employees unless we really need them, even if it is for the fire department," closed Maxwell defiantly. The council approved the delay.

"Are you sure about the sampling question?" Chuck asked Nina as they left the council chambers.

"Sure. No problem. Samples are actually very accurate, if done right."

"Well, do it right, then!" said Chuck as he went into his office.

"Yes, sir!" said Nina, with a mock salute. She set about figuring out exactly what she was going to need to do in two months. Six weeks, actually, given that anything she found would need reviews by multiple sets of eyes in the two weeks before the council considered the findings.

One of the most common questions I receive from local government officials is about sampling. A local government would like to conduct a citizen survey and wonders how many people it needs to contact. Or a manager wants to survey employees about a new HR policy and wonders how to get a good sample and what is a sufficient response rate. This section will go over the most important aspects of sampling.

## Getting a good sample

Most people think that samples are simply a small portion of the whole population. Remember: a population is all units of what you are studying, such as all the people in a city, all the students in a school district, or all the states in the country. A sample is a portion of the population; so in that sense, most people are right. However, most people also think that a sample needs to be some set proportion of the population, such as 10% or 20%. Not true! The actual number included in a sample is usually much, much smaller, and it is not a set proportion. However, that small number still can be very, very accurate. Let me explain.

Let's say a city wants to survey citizens about a proposal for a new year-round pool. It wants to use good survey methodology and an adequate sample size to have as good an estimate as possible. The city manager does not want the results to be open to challenge by the local Pool Party Poopers opposition group. The city has 56,000 citizens. The manager, having never read this book, jumps to the conclusion that he would probably need at least 5,000 people in the survey—around 10%—and, therefore, it would cost too much.

> The right sample size depends on three things: precision, confidence, and the spread of the data (dispersion).

The manager would be wrong. There is not a "fixed proportion" rule to follow. A good sample size depends on three main things, two of which the person doing the sampling determines subjectively: precision, confidence, and the spread of the data. You can think of these things as three different limits, or frames, for the sample.

### Frame #1: How precise do you want the estimate to be?

In other words, what is an acceptable margin of error? This is entirely up to the person doing the survey. Any *estimate* is never going to absolutely, totally, completely match the true mean. The estimated average you obtain from your sample will never exactly match the true mean. With samples, researchers must accept the fact they will not find the true value of what they are seeking—whether it's the true average income, the true average height or weight, or the true average opinion. Therefore, a researcher must set the boundaries of what level of "sloppiness" is acceptable when obtaining an estimate.

We are going to revisit an important concept: the confidence interval. If you remember, you hope that your estimate is close to the true value. How close? If you drew brackets around the estimate, hoping to capture the true value between them—either above or below the value of the estimate—you would draw the brackets close around the estimate if you wanted to be very precise. If you want to give yourself lots of room above and below your estimated value, you would allow yourself a larger margin of error—a farther set of brackets—around your estimate.

The larger the acceptable margin of error, the smaller the sample can be—and vice versa. This is logical. If you want a more precise estimate and you are not going to give yourself a lot of wiggle room, you will need more information. More information means more observations in your sample.

***Level of precision: Margin of error.***     The level of precision you want, or the margin of error that is acceptable, is expressed in terms of what is being measured. If you are measuring income, for example, your margin of error needs to be expressed in terms of dollars. Do you want to come up with an estimate of average income? If so, do you want your acceptable margin or the brackets around your estimate, to be plus or minus $1,000? Or do you want your brackets to be plus or minus $5,000 around your estimate? If the former, you would take your sample, calculate the average, and then say, "According to this sample, average income is *x*-dollars, plus or minus $1,000." In other words we estimate that the true value is somewhere in that range. If we use the larger frame, we would say, "According to this sample, average income is *x*-dollars, plus or minus $5,000."

Obviously, the narrower brackets are better from the point of view of the person reading about and using the information, because he or she wants the estimate to be as focused, as precise, as possible. But from the researcher's point of view, that is much harder because it requires a larger sample. From a consumer's point of view, the wider brackets may seem sloppy and much too broad. But from a researcher's point of view, they are much easier because they allow for more flexibility and a smaller sample. This tug-of-war is unavoidable. In most circumstances, you can't have both a small sample and high precision with your estimate.

> If you insist on a very precise estimate, you will need a very large sample. You can't get around it.

Another common way to measure margin of error is in percentages. If you want to survey your local government's population to get an estimate of the proportion of people who own dogs, you will be looking for an estimate measured in percentages. For example, is the population of dog owners only 10% of the population, or is it 35%? This could make a big difference to you if you are considering recommending a new leash law! Just as with dollars, the more precise you wish your estimate to be, the larger your sample will need to be. In this case, you must decide if you want an estimate that allows for a margin of error of 1 percentage point, 3 percentage points, or 5 percentage points.

Be careful how you speak of your margin of error. If you are speaking of margin of error for an estimate of a percentage, such as percentage of the population that owns dogs, your margin of error is usually expressed in percentage points, *not* percent. If your estimate is 50%, a 3-*percentage-point* margin of error would be 50% +/– 3 percentage points. A three *percent* margin of error would be 50% +/– .03 (0.50), or in other words, + or – 3% of 50%.

### Frame #2: How confident do you want to be in your results?

In the previous chapter, we introduced the idea of *confidence* and talked about three levels of confidence that are commonly used: 90%, 95%, and 99%. If you want to be conservative and only accept conclusions that are very, very likely to be accurate, your results would have to meet the threshold of a 99% confidence level. If you are not as strict and, given the question at hand, are willing to set the bar a bit lower as long as you still get results that are very likely to be accurate, you'd use a 90% or 95% confidence level.

Remember that confidence (your percentage of certainty that you are drawing the right conclusion) is different from precision (your acceptable margin of error, plus or minus, around your estimate)! You might be okay with a loose level of precision and therefore a larger margin of error, but you want to be 99.9% confident that you are drawing the right conclusion from your data. You may also want a very precise estimate but are comfortable with a 95% confidence level. The two things are different. Combined, they can have a major impact on your prospective sample size. Think about it. If you tolerate only a very small margin of error (very precise) and want to be 99.9% confident in your results, then both choices require more information and thus a large sample. If you are willing to have a less precise estimate and only need to be 90% confident in your results, then you can settle for a smaller sample.

Now, how does this reasoning fit into determining our sample size? *Just like with our margin of error, our choice of confidence level will determine whether we need a*

### Table 7-1   Levels of precision, confidence levels, and sample size

| Standard for drawing conclusion from analysis | Precision/Margin of Error | Confidence level | Sample size |
|---|---|---|---|
| High standard | 1 to 2 percentage points for estimating a proportion; low margin for a value (example, $3,000 for an estimate of annual income) | 99% | Large (1000+) |
| Medium standard | 2 to 3 percentage points for estimating a proportion; medium margin for a value (example, $5,000 for an estimate of annual income) | 95% | Medium (500-1000) |
| Low standard | 3 to 4 percentage points for estimating a proportion; high margin for a value (example, $10,000 for an estimate of annual income) | 90% | Small (300-500) |

*large sample or can get by with a smaller sample.* It makes sense: If we want to be very confident about our conclusions, say 99% confident, we will want more information and thus a larger sample size. If being 90% confident is sufficient for the task, we can get by with a smaller sample size. Generally, analysts go for the middle on both. They rely on a moderate margin of error—say, 2 or 3 percentage points—and a 95% confidence level.

All of this might be confusing since there are different choices for precision, confidence level, and sample size. The table above may help. Remember that you can pick and choose for two of the three of the options of precision and confidence level and sample size. For example, you may adopt a medium standard for precision, a high for confidence and as a result, have to obtain a high standard for the sample size. Or you may have no choice but a low standard for a sample size and an externally set margin of error, which in turn will limit the confidence level you can achieve.

### Frame #3: How spread out are your data?

The one thing in determining sample size that does not depend on your preference is the spread of the distribution of your data. Again, once you think about it, it is logical. If everyone in the whole city of Pittsburgh were 5'7" tall, you would not need a large sample to come up with an estimate of Pittsburghers' average height: 5'7". If you measured ten people for your sample, the average would be 5'7". If you added ten more people, the average would still be 5'7".

Let's expand the range of height of the Pittsburghers a little and say that the whole city is between 5'5" and 5'9" tall, in a normal distribution. Let's pretend that the true estimate is still 5'7". You could measure ten people, and the sample estimate may be just a little off—say, 5'6". If you added one more person, your estimate would move, but only slightly, toward the true mean. The additional person does not change the estimate very much. *Since everyone in Pittsburgh is about the same height, you don't need a big sample to get a good estimate of average height!*

But what if your data are really spread out? What if people in Pittsburgh measure anywhere from 3' to 7' tall? If you measured ten people at random, you might end up with an average height estimate that is 5'7" 6'3" or 4'5". If you added ten more people to your sample, the average you calculate can change a lot relative to what you are measuring. One very short person or one very tall person could shift the sample mean quite a bit. It takes a lot more observations to settle on an estimate that does not shift much with the addition of one person. It is at that point that you are close to the true mean. The point of all this is that if your population data are very varied, with a wide distribution, you will need a larger sample in order to have a good sample. If your population data are very similar, with a tighter distribution, you can use a smaller sample size.

### Sample size and standard deviation

How do we incorporate this reasoning into sample size? With standard deviation of the population. Remember how the standard deviation measures the spread of our data? If the standard deviation is small relative to the mean, the data are tightly clustered around the mean. If the standard deviation is large relative to the mean, the data are *not* tightly clustered around the mean. If you need to remind yourself of what they would look like, refer back to the Figures 6–1 and 6–2 of a wide distribution and a narrow distribution, respectively.

Now comes the statement that everyone makes at this point: well, if I knew the standard deviation of the population, then I would also know the true average of the population and I wouldn't need a sample in the first place!!! Arrrgghhh! This is true. And for determining your sample size you won't have the standard deviation of the population. So we have to use something that is a good guess.

One way to get a good guess is to use the standard deviation of data from a similar data set. Let's say, for example, that I want to sample people in Austin, Texas, to determine the average income in the city. If I need the standard deviation to figure out what sample size is appropriate, I might look at data from the previous year in Austin or at data from another city, such as San Antonio. Of course, these data are not going to be a perfect match, but all I need is a good guess.

Another option is to **presample.** This is where the analyst might start the research by taking a small sample first, determining its standard deviation, and using that standard deviation as the guess. Or you might simply make your best guess, and use **sensitivity analysis** to determine what seems reasonable. Sensitivity analysis means that you would change your guess several times, plug the values into the formula to determine recommended sample sizes, and see how sensitive the result is to your changes.

### The formula for sample size

Did I say "formula?" Yes! Yes, a simple formula brings these three components together:

$$\left( \frac{t\text{-score associated with the chosen confidence level} \times \text{standard deviation guess}}{\text{Acceptable margin of error}} \right)^2.$$

To calculate the appropriate sample size for your study, you only need to plug in the values for these three components—the *t*-score associated with the chosen confidence level, the standard deviation guess, and the chosen acceptable margin of error—and *square the result.* If you are familiar with math, you'll see that on the top, the higher the confidence level, the higher the *t*-score and the higher the resultant sample size. In the same vein, the higher the standard deviation guess, the higher the resultant sample size. On the bottom, the higher the acceptable margin of error, the lower the resultant sample size. Let's walk through an example of estimating a sample size:

Let's say we want to survey the citizens of Traer, Iowa, to ask about their satisfaction with public safety. We'll ask them to rate their satisfaction on a scale from

0 to 100, with 0 being entirely dissatisfied and 100 being completely satisfied in all respects. We can't survey everyone because Traer is too large, so we need to take a sample instead. But how big should the sample be? We can use the formula.

First, we would fall back on the standard confidence level used in most analyses, 95%, and from that we know to use the associated *t*-score of 1.96. Where could we go to get a standard deviation to use in our estimate for a good survey size? Let us assume that the nearby town of Toledo, Iowa, used the same survey last year. So let's steal from them. The standard deviation from Toledo last year was 17 points. Traer's city council is fussy, and it wants the margin of error to be only plus or minus 2 points. Here is a summary of the information that we need:

Confidence level: 95%
Associated *t*-score: 1.96
Guessed standard deviation: 17 points
Acceptable margin of error: 2 points

What do you get if you plug these values into the formula? Try it. I got a recommended sample size of 278.

$$\left( \frac{1.96 \times 17}{2} \right)^2$$

## Choosing sample size

After all this explanation, I hope you see that "appropriate sample size" is really a subjective decision of the researcher combined with the nature (spread or distribution) of the underlying data—with one major exception. Even if you're seeking high confidence and a low margin of error and the data seem to have a high standard deviation, once a sample size reaches around 1,000 or so, it will be large enough for most studies. Why? Because even though your choices seem to require a higher sample size, after about 1,000 observations, additional observations will not affect the estimate very much, so going for a larger and larger sample is not really worth the effort. In fact, when analysts use a 95% confidence level, the standard, acceptable sample size is 350 to 450! This is why major national surveys need only a small number of people! If I want to determine presidential approval ratings, I don't have to ask a million people across the United States, even though our population is, at the time of this writing, well over 300 million. I need only several hundred people at a minimum, and maybe a thousand or so at most!

In fact, if I gather more and more data, I may end up with a sample that shows small patterns or differences that are statistically significant but not materially significant. Researchers working with huge data sets can actually be encumbered because they can see the detail in everything, which makes it difficult to identify the truly important relationships.

> At most, to get a good estimate, you need a sample of only about 1,000 for a population of 100 million. We just aren't that different.

Let's consider an example that pulls all these concepts together. In most newspapers that show polls about upcoming elections and the popularity of candidates, a note at the bottom or to the side of the poll gives the details about the methodology and all the assumptions underlying the survey. On July 29, 2009, a *New York Times* poll showed President Obama with a 58% approval rating. That is, when asked if they approved of what Obama was doing as president, 58% of respondents agreed. Here is the detail of the methodology of the poll, as printed in the paper:

### How the poll was conducted

The latest New York Times/CBS News poll is based on telephone interviews conducted July 24 through July 28 with 1,050 adults throughout the United States.

A computer randomly selected the sample of landline telephone exchanges called from a complete list of more than 69,000 active residential exchanges across the country. The exchanges were chosen to ensure that each region of the country was represented in proportion to its population.

Within each exchange, random digits were added to form a complete telephone number, thus permitting access to listed and unlisted numbers alike. Within each household, one adult was designated by a random procedure to be the respondent for the survey.

To increase coverage, respondents reached through random dialing of cell phone numbers was supplemented by this landline sample. The two samples were then combined.

The combined results have been weighted to adjust for variation in the sample relating to geographic region, sex, race, Hispanic origin, marital status, age and education. In addition, the land-line respondents were weighted to take account of household size and number of telephone lines into the residence, while the cell phone respondents were weighted according to whether they were reachable only by cell phone or also by land line.

In theory, in 19 cases out of 20, overall results based on such samples will differ by no more than three percentage points in either direction from what would have been obtained by seeking to interview all American adults. For smaller subgroups, the margin of sampling error is larger. Shifts in results between polls over time also have a larger sampling error.

In addition to sampling error, the practical difficulties of conducting any survey of public opinion may introduce other sources of error into the poll. Variation in the wording and order of questions, for example, may lead to somewhat different results.[1]

The margin of error that the surveyors chose to use was plus or minus 3 percentage points. The newspaper doesn't explicitly say so, but the confidence level chosen was 95%. I know this because the article states: "In theory, in 19 cases out of 20,

---

1   Reprinted with permission from "How the Poll Was Conducted," *New York Times*, July 29, 2009, http://www.nytimes.com/2009/07/30/us/politics/30mbox.html?_r = 1 (accessed March 3, 2010).

overall results based on such samples will differ by no more than three percentage points in either direction from what would have been obtained by seeking to interview all American adults." In theory, this also means that in 1 out of 20 cases, or in 5% of the cases, the estimated approval rating from the survey would fall outside of the margin of error; in other words, the conclusion from the survey would be wrong. We can be 95% confident that Obama's true approval rating, on the day of the survey, was somewhere between 55% and 61% (3 percentage points above and below our sample mean of 58%).

## Response rates

The question "what is a good response rate?" is the kind of question that frustrates both the questioner and the responder. The answer is: "It depends." Response rates have to be considered in the context of the survey and the sample of people answering it. A wide range of factors can increase or decrease what you would consider a good response rate. For example, if you are targeting a group traditionally overwhelmed with requests, you can expect a lower response rate—for instance, from elected officials or from the manager in a university town. Between UNC Chapel Hill, North Carolina State, and Duke University, local government officials in the area have been surveyed and interviewed to death. Other factors are as follows:

- If you are targeting a group of incredibly busy people, you can expect a lower response rate. I understand from a business professor that researchers targeting stockbrokers would be thrilled with a 10% response rate.
- If you have a positive long-term professional relationship with the group and the survey relates to a relevant issue, you can expect a much higher response rate. The faculty member I work with on surveys to city planners can easily get an 80% response rate on the first try.
- If the survey is long, the response rate will go down.
- If the survey includes some incentive, from a pencil to a $20 gift card, the response rate will go up.
- If the survey asks for information that is not readily available (I call this the "do I have to get out of my chair" factor), the response rate goes down.
- If the survey takes more than 2–3 minutes to complete, response rates will go down.
- If the survey asks for personal information, the response rate will go down.
- If the group is more educated, the response rate will be higher.
- If the group is older, the response rate will be higher.
- If you use the official letterhead of a sponsoring organization, the response rate will go up.
- And so on. . . .

In general, the higher the response rate, the better. You always try to get the highest response rate you can. Recent research has shown, however, that extra efforts to bring in those last few surveys are not worth it. The results generally do not change; the same conclusions can be drawn from the lower, immediate response rate. The additional surveys that trickle in at the end don't add much. And in the end, you have to stop trying and just do your analysis with what you have.

So given all these factors, a low response rate (say 10% to 40%) can be good if that is what is normal for that particular context. That does not mean the low response rate is problem-free. The lower the response rate, the more you have to worry about nonresponse bias. Nonresponse bias happens when there is a systematic difference between those who responded and those who didn't. For example, did only the elected officials who were Democrats respond to the survey about environmental legislation? Did only older citizens in town complete the entire, long, citizen satisfaction survey? If you have a lower response rate, you have to ask yourself whether the folks who answered are somehow different from the folks who did not. The easiest way to check for nonresponse bias is to look at who responded. For example, do there seem to be far more responses from the eastern part of town? Did only bigger cities respond to the survey about use of capital budgeting? There are additional ways to detect nonresponse bias, but they involve far more formulas than this book allows.

> ## Random sampling is the gold standard in surveying. Always go with random sampling unless you absolutely, positively need to do otherwise.

A few other things are interesting about the *New York Times* poll in 2009. Obviously, the pollsters were concerned about who was represented in the sample. If a sample is chosen completely at random, every person in the population has an equal chance of being included. And it is likely that the resulting sample will include about the same proportion of men, women, African Americans, whites, Asians, etc., that are in the entire population. But if you want to make sure that there is an equal proportion, you can break your sample into those groups and randomly sample within them (called **stratified sampling,** as in taking a sample of dirt from different strata in a rock face). Another option is to weigh the responses of people in a particular group so that their collective response has the same relative impact as their group in the population. That is, you can make the response of an African American carry more importance in estimating the survey results, if you want. This type of manipulation of the sample is best left to professional surveyors, but educated consumers of survey information should know for whom the survey is speaking. Remember that anytime you try to construct a sample rather than have it chosen at random from the population, you introduce bias.

## Surveys and cell phones

The *New York Times* article also mentions that the survey was done via telephone, and it highlights one of the biggest problems with survey methodology today: cell phones. Traditional telephone surveys are done by randomly calling people with phones. It was easy enough to get phone numbers from the phone directories. We have known for a long time that this excludes those without phones and those with unlisted numbers—a relatively small proportion of the overall population. But there is no directory of cell phone numbers. If I tried to follow the traditional telephone methodology, paying a company to provide me with a random list of numbers in a particular area code, the number of people without landline phones would grow, and young adults would be excluded almost entirely. In my most recent graduate statistics course, out of 30 students, only 2 had landline phones.

You might think that simply choosing numbers at random would be easy, and it would capture both landlines and cell phones. But think about the costs involved in surveying. Every phone call to a nonexistent, commercial, or disconnected line takes time, and time is money. Establishing a random list of numbers to call would include a sizable proportion of bad numbers. The problem is extreme if you have a specific group that you want to survey, such as teens who use the local swimming pool. How are you going to locate all the cell phone numbers from which you could draw a random sample? Just dialing numbers at random and hoping you catch a teen that has been to the local pool would be a tremendous waste of time. The *New York Times* poll explains how it tries to get around this problem: by using landlines for most of the survey and cell phones for part of it. It is as good an effort as one can make, but as cell phone use continues to grow in our country, the problem will only get worse.

The art (not science) of gathering information that is valid and reliable needs to evolve with technology and social trends. Recently, I advised a nonprofit on how to reach former college-scholarship recipients. We were unsuccessful in locating contact information for a number of the former students. However, an inspired survey director decided to locate them via Facebook. I established a Facebook page for the purposes of contacting the students and was able to reach three more within twenty-four hours.

## Estimates, not reality

I'll end on an important point. All samples have a margin of error, and we tend to ignore it. But you shouldn't forget that the margin of error is there. Analysts never really can give an exact estimate; they should always report a range—the average plus or minus the margin of error—and make sure that the audience knows the range. This comes up when, in political races, polls show two candidates with support percentages that are close together. If a poll shows that Candidate A has support of 48% of the electorate and Candidate B has support of 50% of the electorate, and if you like Candidate B, you might think yay, we're winning! But don't be too confident. With a 3% margin of error, the true value for candidate A could be between 45% and 51%, and the true value for candidate B could be between 47% and 53%. Those two ranges overlap. If the true value for Candidate A were 51% and the true value for Candidate B were 49%, all those celebratory Candidate B supporters would be very disappointed when the actual results came in. Don't confuse all polls, or all samples, with reality. They are only *estimates!*

## "Here are the last of the paper surveys. Couldn't we have just done this

some easier way?" Sharon was crabby. She had been recruited into helping input survey data and was not happy about having to step away from her end-of-year accounting preparation. Council Top had decided that as long as it was going to survey its volunteer firefighters, it might as well contact other jurisdictions to see if they wanted to participate.

In the end, the city had sampled 400 volunteer firefighters from around the entire southwest corner of the state. About half, 205, had responded quickly to the e-mail request to go to the survey web page, which recorded those surveys automatically and immediately.

Nina was thrilled with how easy it was. The formatting was easy. So was creating the questions and controlling the answer selection. For example, she really wanted to know what people thought about their volunteer firefighter experience, so she did not want to let respondents have the option of answering "neutral," or three on a seven-point scale. So she allowed the survey to include only "very positive," "positive," "somewhat positive," "somewhat negative," "negative," and "very negative." And . . . it was free! She only had to pay if she wanted some special analyses done.

The jurisdictions involved had many members without e-mail addresses, or if the firefighter had one, the jurisdiction did not have it on record in any central location. But all of them had addresses that Nina could easily track through the water billing system. So in addition to sending out a notice to those with e-mail addresses, Nina sent out postcards with the web address for the survey; and then she finally sent out a follow-up mailing to those who had still not responded; it included the survey and a self-addressed stamped envelope and a free "Firefighters Are Hot" bumper sticker. She knew that any type of incentive would increase response rates: people felt too guilty about getting something for nothing to ignore the request to return the survey. The paper surveys came in much slower, and Sharon had been working at inputting the responses from them.

"We ended up with 87 paper surveys. None has come in for six days. Do you want me to keeping checking the mailroom?" Sharon clearly did not want to have to check with the mailroom again.

"No, we have to cut off the responses at some point so we can start the analysis. And adding the 87 to our original 205, we have 292 total. That is 292 out of 400 . . . a response rate of 73%. That's fantastic!" Nina could hardly contain her excitement.

Sharon looked at her for a moment, half laughed, half snickered, and said, "Well, I'm glad someone is excited about this. Didn't you have to throw out a bunch?"

"Yeah, you're right. The overall response rate was 73%, but we had to throw out the ones from retired firefighters. Whether they were satisfied with their work situation fifteen years ago doesn't help us much now."

"How did they get mixed in?" Sharon sat down.

"Some towns added new volunteers to their rolls but never cleaned off the names of people who no longer were volunteers. You would think that it would be easy to pull together a list of current volunteer firefighters and their contact information, but fewer than half the towns could do it. The others all had problems. It took me three weeks to clean up the list, and even then, many bad names or contact information got through. If you throw out the retirees and look at only usable surveys, the response rate goes down to 54%. But that is still really good."

"Can you mix the results from the paper surveys and the electronic surveys? Is that against the rules or something?"

"Actually, if we were doing scientific research of the highest standard, we probably wouldn't want to mix the results since people who respond electronically are different in a systematic way from those who respond to paper surveys. But for our purposes, it shouldn't be a big problem. We can compare the responses from the two groups and see if there is a difference, and if there is, we can see whether it is big enough to really matter. If there is a difference, I bet it is due to age. We ask people's age, so we'll be able to test that hypothesis."

Sharon stood up. "Do you need me anymore?" Her interest in survey methodology was clearly waning.

"Uh, no. Thank you very much, Sharon."

"Sure. Anytime." Sharon disappeared down the hallway. Nina suspected that Sharon would stop at the smoking spot outside the back of the building on her way back to her desk. She turned back to the computer. Setting up and running the survey had taken four weeks. She only had a week in which to produce the draft report. She had already prepared the intro, background, and methodology sections while waiting for the survey results. She just needed to plug in the results, conclusions, and recommendations and write an executive summary. Plenty of time.

## Review questions

1. What are the three frames by which to determine an adequate sample size?

2. What is a margin of error? How does a small margin of error affect the sample size?

3. If you want to obtain a very precise estimate, how would that affect your margin of error and sample size?

4. Create your own example to determine an appropriate sample size. Use the formula provided.

5. What are the benefits of a large sample size? What are the possible drawbacks?

6. Describe three possible alternatives to using landline telephones to conduct surveys, and explain how each might affect your response rate.

   a.

   b.

   c.

7. What is stratified sampling, and when might you use this technique?

8. Which of these three options is the most appropriate way to determine an adequate sample size? Explain why the others are inappropriate.

   a. Take 10% of the population and use that number.

   b. Use the three frames to determine the sample size.

   c. Look at other research on the topic and use the same sample size.

9. Describe the relationship between precision and margin of error. Why is it important when sampling a population?

10. Look at the article about the survey taken to determine President Obama's approval rating. What can you assume about the margin of error, precision, and overall reliability and validity of this survey?

# Can We PLEASE Start to Actually Conclude Something?

## [ DRAWING CONCLUSIONS WITH NOMINAL OR ORDINAL DATA ]

**"I'm not sure what to do with this survey data."** The summer intern appeared at Nina's cubicle entrance (it couldn't really be called a door).

Nina took a deep breath before turning around. The intern was really, really trying to be helpful, but Nina was wondering if having an intern was actually a help or if she should add a new line, "hand-holder," under her own job description. No, if she complained to Chuck, he would probably laugh and say it would just fit under "and other duties as assigned." She should have asked that that line be taken off the description before she accepted the job offer.

What was she thinking?! She loved this job. And the intern really wasn't that bad; in fact, she asked great questions and had already suggested new ways to present data to the council. It was just that she worked so quickly that as soon as Nina gave her one job, she seemed to be done within minutes, asking for the next task.

"We need to put the data into some tables to see if there are differences between professional and volunteer firefighters. Let me see if I can show you an example." Nina started searching her computer file folders for some old electronic files.

"Do you mean some cross tabs?" asked Maria.

"Yes!" Nina spun around. "Are you familiar with how to set those up?" Wow! The intern knew about contingency tables. Maria had even used the more casual term of cross tabs, short for cross tabulations! Things were looking up.

"Sure, we worked with lots of qualitative data in my research assistantship. Do you want chi squares run, too?"

"Yes!" Nina squeaked. She couldn't keep the excitement out of her voice. "It would be such a big help if you could run contingency tables for each survey question. I know it will take a long time to do each one, but I also know that some council member sometime, somewhere, will want to know how the responses to each question break down between volunteers and professional firefighters. I would rather be prepared with all the results than not have the answer at the meeting. Otherwise we end up delaying decisions for yet another week while we run more and more numbers."

Maria was almost a little smug in her response. "Actually, you can run all the cross tabs . . . er . . . contingency tables," using the more formal term when she saw Nina's face wince slightly, "at the same time with an option in the stats software we use in our grad program. It will only take a couple of minutes. I'll run them, and then after lunch we can sit down and go over the ones that are statistically significant."

"Now I'm really feeling old." Nina was starting to hate Maria. "Maybe I should think about getting that software. It takes for-ev-er in my spreadsheet program."

"It's a student license. The full license is rather expensive, I think. It would probably be cheaper to just keep hiring student interns," laughed Maria as she stepped away to her own cubicle.

*But could I keep up with them?* thought Nina.

Sometimes it is hard to keep up with how all this information fits together. Let me review where we started in this book, where we are, and what is coming in these last two chapters.

## Where have we been?

We started out with research design in general and talked about the importance of developing a good research design. I outlined eight steps to move you from a general research topic to a general research question, and then to a specific research question.

Step 1: Understand the issue.
Step 2: Identify the problem.
Step 3: Explain your theory.
Step 4: Formulate the research question.
Step 5: Formulate the hypothesis.
Step 6: Operationalize the hypothesis.
Step 7: Select the methodology.
Step 8: Evaluate the data.

### Hypothesis and research design

Within these steps, we talked about building a hypothesis that we can test with data. Ah, the data! Before we even got to a fact or a number, there was so much to talk about concerning data! So much, in fact, that we discussed data all the way into Chapter 2. We talked about the difficulty of operationalizing a concept into nominal, ordinal, and/or interval data that we can measure and summarize in some way.

We wrapped up the eight steps with the two key concepts in research design: (1) validity: are we measuring what we want to measure (i.e., the idea of accuracy)? and (2) reliability: is our design good enough to replicate so that different researchers doing the same study would get the same results (i.e., the idea of consistency? The concept of *validity* is especially important. We want to make sure that we are testing the right relationship or answering the right question for our needs. We also learned how to apply the concept of validity to a measure as much as to the research design. When we measure a concept with data, we need to ask if our chosen measure is really measuring what we want it to measure. For example, if you want to measure how "rich" someone is, should you use income, assets, and net worth? What is considered "income?"

## Collecting and describing data

Then in Chapters 3 and 4, we jumped right in and discussed collecting data and describing them through descriptive statistics by learning how to answer basic questions like: What is a "typical" value in our data (measures of central tendency: mean, median, and mode)? How spread out are our data (measures of dispersion)? Is there anything weird about the data (outliers, skew), and if so, can we still use the data in further analysis? (The answer is yes, through the beauty of the normal curve and, as we learned in Chapter 6, the central limit theorem.) How can I understand where a single point is relative to the rest of the data ($z$-scores and associated percentages)?

If we have a complete population of data, we can stop right there. It is what it is. There are no guesses, no likelihoods, no doubts, no concept of statistical significance. But how often do we have every piece of information for our research question? Not often, as we learned. Starting in Chapter 5 we left "population" behind. Chapters 5, 6, and 7 taught us the reasons we usually use samples, and that with sampling comes uncertainty since we have only estimates and sample error on which to base our analysis. To understand this uncertainty, we had to discuss probability, confidence, and statistical significance.

## Probability, confidence, and statistical significance

These three concepts—probability, confidence, and statistical significance—must be understood if you want to move to one of the most basic questions in any kind of statistical analysis: Is there a difference between this and that? Is there a difference between a sample and the population? Is there a big difference between a single point or observation and the rest of the data? Is there a difference between two groups or samples? These questions are at the heart of inferential statistics, where we use $t$-scores instead of $z$-scores, have confidence intervals around our estimates, and decide on the confidence level we need to reach before we feel safe enough to draw conclusions. Inferential statistics allow us to infer something about a population from the data we have in hand in a sample. (Remember: *to infer* is just a fancy way of saying to guess, to estimate, or to conclude.)

> ## Research is simply asking if there is a difference between this and that.

The first of these concepts is *probability*. In Chapter 5, we learned how a probability is just a ratio, a percentage, a fraction, and how there are a number of ways in which you can obtain a particular outcome over all the possible outcomes. Probability is key to inferential statistics because, since probability is a guess or an estimate, there is *always* a chance that our guess or estimate is wrong. We need to understand basic probability in order to understand the likelihood that our guess, estimate, or conclusion is right or, conversely, that it is wrong.

The second concept, *confidence*, is the natural next step. In Chapter 6, we learned there are two ways analysts use confidence: with confidence intervals and with confidence levels.

Confidence intervals are the same as margins of error. With samples, we are making estimates, right? And we know that the estimates are not perfect; we hope that the real value is somewhere close to our estimate. So we explicitly place brackets around our estimate to mark the level of error that we are comfortable accepting. This is a subjective decision (and gets easier to make, the more we practice). Are we comfortable estimating average income and giving ourselves a margin of error of plus or minus $5,000? Or is that too broad? Would we be more comfortable with an estimate that has a margin of error of plus or minus only $1,000? What we decide will help us determine our sample size.

Confidence levels are also determined subjectively. Once we know how likely it is that we are right (or wrong) when we determine $t$-scores and $p$ values, we can express our level of confidence in our result. Confidence is not just the measure of the likelihood of being right or wrong in our estimate. It is also the standard we choose to apply to the probabilities. This is where judgment and subjectivity come in, and suddenly we realize that the field of statistics can be as open to personal interpretation as art or music.

How much evidence is enough to draw a conclusion and make a decision? How sure do you need to be in your estimate? The same numerical probability of being right or wrong can be acceptable to one analyst, who draws a conclusion that $x$ is different from $y$, and not acceptable to another, who draws the conclusion that there is not enough evidence to say that $x$ is different from $y$. It all depends on the standard of confidence, or the confidence level, that the analyst applies.

Sometimes, when you have a difficult but important policy question, such as the impact of youngsters' home situations on their long-term educational outcomes; you might be willing to accept a lower standard of confidence simply because the cause-and-effect relationship is very difficult to disentangle from other relationships. One researcher may accept a lower level of confidence simply to be able to advance programs. Another researcher may want to apply a higher standard, requiring a higher level of confidence before making any policy decisions or changes. (Remember: We are always talking about a relatively high level of confidence in all cases. The choice is usually between using a standard level of 90%, 95%, or 99% confidence.)

The third concept, *statistical significance*, introduced at the end of Chapter 6, feeds off of confidence. If we come up with results that meet our 90%, 95%, or 99.9% level of confidence, we can say the results are statistically significant. The idea of *significance* has a special meaning to researchers. This conversation might help:

Speaker: "Since we designated Friday night as pizza night at the volunteer stations, the decline in performance has been significant."

Volunteer firefighter: "What do you mean by 'significant?'"

Speaker: "Well, it declined from here," pointing to a middle point on the graph, "to here," pointing to a lower point further across the graph.

Volunteer firefighter: "That's not much of a change to me, actually, when you look at the whole graph. Is it a statistically significant difference?"

Speaker: "What do you mean?"

Volunteer firefighter: "Performance scores go up and down with every test. You never get the same score twice. How do you know this tick down isn't just random?"

Speaker: "Well, I don't."

Volunteer firefighter: "So you are not 95% confident in your conclusion based on these data?"

Speaker (speaking in a very annoyed tone): "No."

Volunteer firefighter: "Well, I suggest we keep Friday night pizza nights until you have enough data to be 95% confident that you are finding a statistically significant drop in performance, as you are implying."

## Where are we now, and where are we going?

We are now at the point where we go beyond asking if there is a difference between this and that. We are now asking if one thing is related to another. In other words, is there some tie between how one thing behaves and how another behaves? We have danced around this question already in this book. We have asked whether there is a link between weather and weapons in Iraq and whether there is a link between professional status and fire deaths. We are entering the world of testing for associations and, eventually, causal relationships.

We will first do this with just two variables—two series of data about something, like the number of rainy days (first thing) and the number of guns found at military checkpoints (second thing). But nothing in life is that easy. Relationships, whether between people or data, are much more complicated. By the end of this book, we will be looking at relationships between two series of data while controlling for other things going on at the same time. We will be able to separate out the impact of something like rainy days from everything else that might be affecting the number of guns at a checkpoint.

How are we going to do this? PATTERNS! Statistics (and for that matter, most research) are simply based on **patterns** in data related to certain associations or co-movement among the data points or observations. Usually we are looking for patterns that are similar to, or in direct contrast with, one another. We are now at the point where we can test the hypotheses we formulated in Step 5 of the research design process! Aren't you excited?! Okay, maybe I expect too much from people who are less geeky than I am. But what this does mean is that we are at the point where we can come up with some results, and for most people, that is an exciting time.

### Association and co-movement

It is important to distinguish here between association and causal relationships, and to review some material that we introduced in Chapter 1. There, we talked about models of how different variables relate to each other. We are going to return to those models because we are now at the point where we can actually test our hypotheses!

An **association** is weaker than a relationship (just as an acquaintanceship is less strong than a friendship). An association means that there is co-movement between the variables: when one moves, so does the other. There are two kinds of co-movement: positive and negative.

With a positive association, the two variables move in the same direction. That is, when one variable goes up, the other one goes up. When one goes down, the other one goes down. When the values in one variable increase, then the values in the other variable also increase. The values don't have to increase by the same amount or at the same rate; it is the pattern of movement that matters. The two variables move in concert: ↓↓ ↑↑

With a negative association, the two variables move in opposite directions. That is, when one variable goes up, the other variable goes down. ↓↑ ↑↓

If, when one variable changes, there is no change in the second, we know that there is no association between the two since there is no movement or change in the second variable.

### Moving from co-movement to causality

Maybe there is an association, but is there causality? That is, just because things move in the same direction does not mean that they are truly linked. Using the example in Chapter 1 of popsicles and the level of murders, we realized that while the amount of popsicle consumption and the number of murders might co-vary—that is, there might be an association where both move in a positive or negative direction together—there is not a **causal relationship** between the two. Remember: to support the claim that one thing affects another—for example, that job-training programs for prison inmates reduce recidivism—you must have four things:

1. Time order

2. Theoretical support

3. Co-variation

4. Legitimacy.

At this point, when we want to actually test to see if a relationship exists, the theory (and model) we developed in Step 3 is particularly important because it helps us identify what we consider the dependent variable and the independent variable(s). The **dependent variable** is the variable that depends on the other variable(s)—go figure! If you were an English major long ago in your college days, it is like the direct object of a sentence: it is the thing being affected. The **independent variables** are what influence or act on the dependent variable. Let's go back to one of the illustrations we had at the beginning of the book.

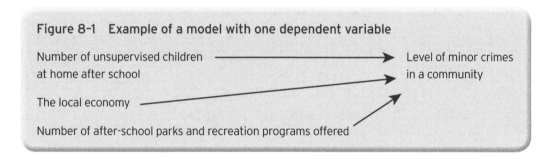

**Figure 8-1   Example of a model with one dependent variable**

Number of unsupervised children at home after school ———————————————→ Level of minor crimes in a community

The local economy ————

Number of after-school parks and recreation programs offered

In this example, the dependent variable is the level of minor crimes in a community. We want to understand what is influencing those crimes. Why are they going up or down? The three factors we have listed—number of unsupervised children at home after school, the local economy, and number of after-school parks and recreation programs offered—are all things that we think influence the minor crime rate. They are all independent variables in this model. They all have arrows going out of them; they are influencing other things. The level of minor crimes is the recipient of the arrows; it is being affected by these other things. There is only one dependent variable in each model. Here, you can look at the relationships one by one, or you can look at all of them at the same time. However, if you draw a model and it looks like Figure 8–2, you are in for more work.

In this example, there are three dependent variables and only one independent variable. Again, you can look at them one by one, but in this case, you can't look at this as a single model. For a single model, we need to have only one dependent variable. Looking at data for this example requires looking at three separate models.

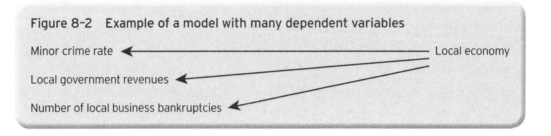

**Figure 8-2   Example of a model with many dependent variables**

Minor crime rate ◄─────────────────────────────── Local economy

Local government revenues ◄───────

Number of local business bankruptcies ◄───────

Let's go back to the first, better model (Figure 8–1). We can now add in our hypotheses about whether the relationship between each independent variable and the dependent variable is positive or negative, as shown in Table 8–1.

**Table 8-1   Variables and hypothesized relationships in model**

| Independent variable | Dependent variable | Hypothesized nature of relationship |
|---|---|---|
| Number of unsupervised children at home after school | Level of minor crime in the community | Positive: As the number of unsupervised children goes up, the level of minor crime goes up. |
| The local economy | Level of minor crime in the community | Negative: As the local economy grows, the level of minor crime in the community decreases. |
| Number of after-school parks and recreation programs offered | Level of minor crime in the community | Negative: As the number of after-school parks and recreation programs offered increases, the level of minor crime in the community decreases. |

Geez, enough review! Can we get to testing for causal relationships already? Yes, we can. Let's get to it.

### Testing for relationships: Nominal and ordinal data

We focus on six guiding questions when testing for relationships and these questions will be the basis for the rest of this book. Together we will walk through common ways to answer them. (The statistical language version is presented first, with the normal English-language translation in parentheses.)

1. Is there an association between the variables?
   *(Is there a consistent pattern in the two sets of data?)*

2. What is the strength of the association?
   *(How strong is the pattern?)*

3. Is one variable having an impact on another? Do you think there may be causality?
   *(Is there a relationship between the two variables?)*

4. What is the direction and nature of that relationship? Which is the dependent and which is the independent variable?
   *(What kind of relationship is it, and what kind of variables are they?)*

5. Is the relationship statistically significant?
   *(Is it statistically significant?)*

6. Is the relationship materially significant?
   *(Does it really matter?)*

## Interpreting results

Let's consider the first question: "Is there a similar pattern in the two sets of data?" The first step in knowing how to answer the question is to understand your data. What kind of data do you have: interval, ordinal, or nominal, or a combination? The methods you use to look for associations and relationships, and the tests you use to understand if those relationships are significant, depend on the nature of the data, as shown in Table 8–2.

**Table 8-2    Types of data and tests used in everyday statistics**

| Kind of data | Method used to look for relationships | Is there a pattern? What is its strength? | Is it significant? | Does it really matter? |
|---|---|---|---|---|
| Interval | Regression | $r$ and $r^2$ | $t$-tests, F-tests | Up to your audience |
| Ordinal | Contingency tables/cross tabs | Gamma, Tau, Somers' D | Chi square ($X^2$) | Up to your audience |
| Nominal | Contingency tables/cross tabs | Lambda, Cramer's V | Chi square ($X^2$) | Up to your audience |

I know I hear a sigh of relief from the reader at this point because you notice at least one letter that is somewhat familiar to you: $t$ as used in $t$-tests. *T*-tests allow us to determine if there is a statistically significant difference, measured by a *t*-score (surprise!) between two things: an observation and the rest of a population, a sample and a population, or two samples. Or is it a gasp I hear, because you think you have to learn about things like Gammas and Lambdas, F-tests, and other letters of the Greek alphabet? Rest assured, dear reader; we will learn about how some of these things work—for example, we will briefly talk about F-scores at the end of Chapter 9—but most statistical software programs do the math for you. Your job is to be able to interpret the results, and luckily, you do so through the lens of *confidence* that we have already covered.

## Association in nominal or ordinal data

For the rest of this chapter, we will focus on how to understand if two things represented by nominal or ordinal data are associated. We will save interval data for Chapter 9.

You may remember from Chapter 2 that nominal data (sometimes called *categorical data*) are data that are represented as members of a group or category. There is no set interval or relative value between the different members. For example, the different flavors of ice cream are categorical data. There is no set value between chocolate, vanilla, butter pecan, or mint chocolate chip. We can only count the members of these groups. Of course, you will be able to count the number of people who prefer vanilla to chocolate, but the actual group of "vanilla" has no numerical value in and of itself.

Remember also that ordinal data are data for which there is not a set value to different groups or a set interval between groups, but you can rank-order the groups. For example, when you do a survey and ask citizens about their level of satisfaction with local government services, you might ask if they are highly satisfied, satisfied, unsatisfied, or very unsatisfied. These categories have a value in relation to each other, but we can't really measure the difference between satisfied and unsatisfied.

If you have either nominal or ordinal data, you analyze relationships with contingency tables. Now the steps:

***Step 1: Determine the independent dependent variables.***   A **contingency table** has one variable listed across the top and another listed down the left side. The first step in setting up a table is go back to your original model and ask yourself which is the dependent variable and which is the independent variable. The independent variable is across the top, comprising the columns. The dependent variable is down the side, comprising the rows. For example, in Table 8–3 the dependent variable is average citizen rating for service quality, and the independent variable is type of solid-waste pickup service.

***Step 2: Set up the contingency table.***   Start with putting in the data frequencies (frequencies are the counts: how many yeses or how many nos, etc.) from the survey results in each cell as appropriate. This produces a contingency table, as shown in Table 8–3.

**Table 8-3**   Contingency table of solid-waste pickup service and citizen satisfaction

| Average citizen rating for service quality | Type of solid-waste pickup service | | |
|---|---|---|---|
| | Backyard pickup | Curbside pickup | Total |
| Satisfied or very satisfied | 300  (86%) | 25  (17%) | 325  (65%) |
| Unsatisfied or very unsatisfied | 50  (14%) | 125  (83%) | 175  (35%) |
| Total | 350  (100%) | 150  (100%) | 500  (100%) |

This table shows the results of a survey of 500 residents in Council Top, Iowa. Council Top has two types of solid-waste pickup service. In the older part of town, backyard pickup has existed for over forty years; yes, believe it or not, in some towns, the solid-waste workers will walk around to the back of the house, carry the bins to the truck, and then return the bins to the back of the house. Newer areas of town, as they have been built, have had to settle for curbside pickup. The manager, Chuck Edwards, wanted to see if there was a way to show his council that citizens with curbside pickup were just as satisfied with solid-waste services as citizens who received backyard pickup. If so, the entire town could be converted to curbside pickup (he hoped with trucks that would have mechanical arms, otherwise known as the "one-armed bandits," which also tend to need only one employee on them instead of two; the savings were so tempting!). While he didn't say so directly, he was really asking if service type (the independent variable) had an impact on satisfaction (the dependent variable).

You may already be able to see that Chuck is going to be disappointed, but let's give him all the numbers and see if there really is a relationship between solid-waste service type and citizen satisfaction.

**Step 3: Convert the frequencies to percentages and compare across rows.**   It can be hard to make good comparisons with raw numbers. To make things easier, we simply convert our data frequencies in Table 8–3 to *percentages*. In this case, the sizes of the two groups are different. There are many more customers served by backyard pickup than by curbside pickup. To **standardize** the numbers so that we can compare them easily, we convert the cells into percentages *going down,* which means that each column totals to 100% In each column, the cells in the table now show the percentages for each category. The percentages can be added as you go down the column to reach 100%.

Table 8–4 shows how we would convert Chuck's table. Now comparisons are

Table 8-4   Cross tab of solid-waste pickup service and citizen satisfaction

| Average citizen rating for service quality | Type of solid-waste pickup service | | |
| --- | --- | --- | --- |
| | Backyard pickup (%) | Curbside pickup (%) | Total (%) |
| Satisfied or very satisfied | 86 | 17 | 65 |
| Unsatisfied or very unsatisfied | 14 | 83 | 35 |
| Total | 100 | 100 | 100 |

much easier. From this table, we can tell Chuck the bad news. We can break the news to him in a variety of ways:

- More than 85% of citizens with backyard pickup are satisfied with their service, compared to only 17% of curbside pickup citizens.

- There is a 69-point difference in the percentage (or in other words, a 69-percentage-point difference) of citizens who are satisfied with backyard pickup compared with those who are satisfied with curbside pickup.

- Backyard pickup customers are over four times more likely to be satisfied with their solid-waste service than curbside pickup customers are.

## Convert into percentages down and compare across.

But perhaps Chuck is not going to bring up the differences after all; if he did, he could end up with all citizens getting backyard pickup! He might just want to emphasize that the majority of citizens, 65%, are happy with their solid-waste service. Without knowing it, Chuck has gone through four of our questions on associations and causality:

1. Is there an association between the variables?
   *(Is there a consistent pattern in the two sets of data?)*

   Based on the contingency tables, it sure seems like there is a pattern in the data Remember: an association means that there is co-movement between the variables: when one moves, so does the other. The variable along the top, type of solid-waste service is nominal. The satisfaction rating data are ordinal. Chuck sees the pattern: as the percentage of one dependent variable goes down (across the first row), the percentage of the other dependent variable goes up (across the second row). The data in the table could also be graphed.

2. What is the strength of the association?
   *(How strong is the pattern?)*

   The strongest association is a perfect association. In statistics, a **perfect association** is one in which one variable is perfectly correlated with another. Huh? That means that if you know one variable, you can predict the other variable with

100% success. They move together perfectly and predictably: if you know the value of one, you know the value of the other. Well, a perfect association to give Chuck nightmares would be one shown in Table 8–5 (percentages in parentheses).

Table 8-5   Example of cross tab of solid-waste pickup service and citizen satisfaction with a perfect relationship

| Average citizen rating for service quality | Type of solid-waste pickup service | | |
|---|---|---|---|
| | Backyard pickup | Curbside pickup | Total |
| Satisfied or very satisfied | 350  (100%) | 0  (0%) | 350  (65%) |
| Unsatisfied or very unsatisfied | 0  (0%) | 150  (100%) | 150  (35%) |
| Total | 350  (100%) | 150  (100%) | 500  (100%) |

The weakest association, on the other hand, is the one where there is no difference (percentages are approximately the same) across the percentages in the different columns of the independent variable, as shown in Table 8–6.

Table 8-6   Example of cross tab of solid-waste pickup service and citizen satisfaction with no relationship

| Average citizen rating for service quality | Type of solid-waste pickup service | | |
|---|---|---|---|
| | Backyard pickup | Curbside pickup | Total |
| Satisfied or very satisfied | 228  (65%) | 98  (65%) | 326  (65%) |
| Unsatisfied or very unsatisfied | 122  (35%) | 52  (35%) | 174  (35%) |
| Total | 350  (100%) | 150  (100%) | 500  (100%) |

Here, it doesn't matter if you have backyard or curbside pickup. In both cases, about two-thirds of the citizens are satisfied and about one-third are not. The statistics called Lambda and Cramer's V and others actually try numerically to measure the strength of the association when using ordinal and nominal data. Those measures are beyond the scope of this book, but they are available in the software programs if you want them. For most purposes in state and local government work, simply comparing the percentages will be enough for your audience.

3. Is one variable having an impact on another? Do you think there may be causality? *(Is there a relationship between the two variables?)*

Chuck has a theory, a hypothesis, that the type of solid-waste service the citizen has and that citizen's satisfaction with the service are not just associated, but related. He really thinks one is causing the other.

4. What is the direction and nature of that relationship? Which is the dependent and which is the independent variable?
*(What kind of relationship is it, and what kind of variables are they?)*

This is a no-brainer. Chuck thinks that the type of service has an influence, or an impact, on service satisfaction. A When the service type changes from curbside to backyard, satisfaction increases. *Service type* is the independent variable; *satisfaction* is the dependent variable.

5. Is the relationship statistically significant?
*(Is it statistically significant?)*

Ah, now we are in new territory. In this book, we already talked about how to determine if two groups were statistically significantly different through *t*-scores. This works for interval data when you are working with samples. Now the question is, how can you do it with nominal or ordinal data? Through a measure called the **chi square.** Chi square compares the actual frequencies in your table with the frequencies you would expect if there were no relationship. For Chuck, it would be comparing the actual data he has in his table with what he would have in the No Relationship example in Table 8–6. Again, the calculations are beyond the scope of this text, but the result is called a *chi square value*. This value is not important in and of itself, but it is associated with a *p* value. YAY! Now we are back to something familiar! Remember how "for every *t*, there is a *p*"? Well, in the same way, for every chi square value, there is an associated *p* value.

The *p* values are interpreted in the same way as before. The *p* value indicates the likelihood that the data would appear the way they do (in other words, the way the data are distributed across the individual cells) if it were due just to random chance. If there were no relationship, could you get a table that looks like this? Think about it. When we get extreme values in any kind of results in research, like flipping a coin a hundred times and only getting one heads, we are suspicious about whether or not we could get the results randomly. We immediately tend to suspect the coin is not fair.

So how do we figure out exactly how likely is it that the data would just randomly appear in the table as they do? Luckily, the computer software programs calculate the *p* values for us when they calculate the chi squares. The higher the chi square value, the lower the *p* value (if you remember, just like the higher the *t*, the lower the *p*). If you are using a 95% confidence level as your standard and you have a *p* value at or below .05, you could say that you are at least 95% confident that there is a relationship between the two variables.

In Chuck's case, the chi square value for Table 8–4 is 220, with an associated *p* value of .000. We can say that there is virtually no chance that Chuck got these survey results at random; in other words, there is virtually *no* chance that there is *no* relationship. In other, other words, we can be 99.9% confident that there *is* a relationship. In fact, we can say with almost 100% confidence that there is a relationship and that the type of solid-waste service does have an influence on citizen satisfaction ratings. All of these sentences are different ways of saying the same thing.

6. Is the relationship materially significant?
*(Does it really matter?)*

Well, to Chuck, it is significant; it does matter. For any researcher, whether something is materially significant is a judgment call. For Chuck, it is clear that backyard pickup is a lot more popular than curbside pickup—and that he is going to be stuck with backyard solid-waste pickup for a long time.

**Table 8-7   Firefighter deaths contingency table**

| Type of duty | Career, no. | Volunteer, no. |
|---|---|---|
| Operating at fire ground | 22 | 12 |
| Responding to or returning from alarm | 4 | 26 |
| Other on duty | 9 | 4 |
| Training | 7 | 5 |
| Operating at nonfire emergencies | 0 | 6 |
| Totals | 42 | 53 |

**Table 8-8   Firefighter deaths cross tab**

| Type of duty | Career, % | Volunteer, % |
|---|---|---|
| Operating at fire ground | 52 | 23 |
| Responding to or returning from alarm | 10 | 49 |
| Other on duty | 21 | 8 |
| Training | 17 | 9 |
| Operating at nonfire emergencies | 0 | 11 |
| Totals | 100 | 100 |

**"What did you find?"** Nina was tired and cranky by the end of the day, but she was trying to shrug it off. She had been working with the budget office all day on a performance measurement report on home inspections, but some of the data were inconsistent with other departmental reports. She didn't understand why the numbers were different, and she had been trying to untangle the mess for hours. She was ready to throw up her hands, close her eyes, pick a report at random, and go with it for the official benchmark numbers.

"Here is the cross tab of the data for the firefighter deaths," said Maria, handing her one piece of paper.

"And here it is with the percentages."

"Is the difference statistically significant? Not that I am going to report that to the council," laughed Nina. "They would look at me as if I had horns on my head. I just want to know for myself."

"I checked it," said Maria. "And no surprise. It is very statistically significant: $p$ equals .0000261. About no chance that you would get these numbers randomly."

"Well, I am not surprised, either. At least something today seems to have gone right the first time. What do you think about this: I will present to council the table with the percentages and show how the percentage of deaths among volunteers *operating at the fire ground* is less than half of that for career people. Of course, there will be some discussion about why. So I've looked into training differences, and the professionals have had a lot more training, so go figure. But I haven't been able to ask about physical differences—if there are age or health or weight differences that might be the reason. Actually, looking at the specific incident reports would tell us a lot."

Maria tipped her head. "Would you have to get past HIPAA [Health Insurance Portability and Accountability Act] rules to access that information?"

"Yeah, maybe. I didn't think about that. A simple analysis can get complicated quickly, can't it?" Nina paused. "Do you know anything about home inspections, Maria?"

"No, but if it is about data, I'm willing to learn," Maria said.

"Here, let me show you what I am trying to figure out," said Nina. Under her breath, she muttered, "I have to get more interns."

## Review questions

1. Explain the difference between co-movement and causality.

2. When looking for relationships, what is the method to use with

    a.  Nominal data?

    b.  Ordinal data?

    c.  Interval data?

3. What kind of data can you use in contingency tables?

4. Why are models important to review when you set up a contingency table?

5. Create an example of a contingency table, with the appropriate kind of variables for rows and columns. Explain why contingency tables are organized in this way.

6. What do we mean by "convert to percentages down and compare across" in interpreting contingency tables?

7. Make up data to fill in the contingency table you made in Question 5, and explain the results in a paragraph.

8. Make up two examples of contingency tables, one showing a strong relationship and one showing a weak relationship.

9. How would you use a chi square value?

10. In Table 8-2 appears the statement that whether a result really matters is up to the audience. What does this mean?

# Okay, Folks, What Is Causing the Problem Here?

[ DRAWING CONCLUSIONS WITH INTERVAL DATA ]

**"Well, that does it!"** Nina was happy, although she shouldn't have been. The home inspection data were terrible, but she and Maria had finally figured out that one of the supervising inspectors had instructed his team to fill out the service reports using the wrong dates. The department was trying to keep track of the time taken to complete home inspections. It had been asked to record the dates of the initial request, first visit, and subsequent visits (if needed), and the date on which the building finally passed inspection. One of the teams seemed to be doing a great job with timeliness; its average completion time for the inspection process was lower than that of any of the other teams by almost four days—"a statistically significant difference," Nina remembered Maria saying. She and Maria wanted to know how this particular team did so well: why was it so different from the rest?

"It's easy to be better when you cook the books!" said Maria when they discovered the problem. It wasn't that the team had actually tried to report inaccurate data; the team had simply misunderstood the definition of "the date of initial request." They were supposed to record the date when the request for an inspection was first made to the department; instead, the wonder team interpreted it as the date when the request was forwarded to the team with an appointment. This allowed them to avoid counting the few days it took for the request to work its way through the department office staff.

"Thanks for all your help on this project, Maria," said Nina. "I really appreciate the time you took to go back and pull all those orders to get the right request dates. That team's scores are now in line with the rest; in fact, they are a little slower than most."

"Why do these inspections take so long to complete?" Maria asked, scrolling through the corrected data. "There are a couple in here that go for over three months. Here is one that took over nine months to be completed!"

"Probably a lot of things: the size of the building, how old it is, the experience of the inspector, the number of fixes that need to be done. Lots of stuff, I guess."

"Hmmm. Some of these long ones are in the same couple of neighborhood developments. Do you think there is something going on there?"

"Maybe, but I don't know how you would sort it all out," replied Nina.

"All this information is in the database, correct? Building characteristics, who inspected them, location, number of initial problems, type of problems?" Maria was still moving the mouse all around the screen.

"Yeah. . . . What are you getting at?"

"Oh, I just wonder if we ran a regression on the data if the builder would pop out as statistically significant."

Regression?! Nina remembered some word like that back in her graduate school statistics class, but her brain had shut down by that point in the semester. She had glided through to the final in her course without having to spend too much brainpower on those chapters.

"What is that again?" Nina tried to sound casual, as if she knew all about regression but just needed a moment to remember.

"We can look at all the various potential influences on the timeliness of inspections together in a multivariate regression. It isolates each of the relationships so that you can see what is statistically significant and what is not, and what kind of impact each variable has," said Maria.

"Oh, yeah, I remember now." Of course, Nina didn't. "If you want to play around with the data, I bet Chuck would be interested. He is really bugged by the never-ending complaints about inspections. If he had some data to show why things take so long, he might be able to get the council off that topic."

"Yeah, and onto rewriting the junk car ordinance!" laughed Maria.

"Or pushing the leash law." Nina's voice went low. "All cats must be on a four-foot leash at all times! And the animal control officers will be issued rulers," she joked in a poor attempt to imitate Chuck's voice. They both started snickering. It was late, and they were getting goofy.

"No, no, I know . . . chickens! That is what he needs to tackle next. Council Top needs a new backyard chicken ordinance. We can have a public hearing and make it open to anyone, especially those who want to bring their own chickens to show how harmless they are."

"No, no, this is better . . . a leash law for in-town chickens!!" Nina and Maria almost collapsed with laughter. "And licenses. All chickens must be licensed with photos! And chipped! They have to be chipped! So that if the chicken crosses the road and doesn't get to the other side, the police can pick it up and the owner can be identified! All police cars will have GPS systems that show little dots all the time of where the chickens are!"

"Wait . . . chicken crosswalks! With lights in the shape of a chicken! That's it!"

"With little crossing buttons down low that they can peck to make the 'walk' light go on!" Nina and Maria were holding their sides now.

Chuck poked his head out of his door to see what was going on. The women stopped, looked at Chuck, and burst out laughing again. Chuck decided to disregard the frivolities and gently closed the door.

I n Chapter 8, we introduced the ideas of association and causality between variables but kept our discussion to nominal and/or ordinal data. In this chapter, we talk about the same ideas for interval data.

You might think that determining whether there is a relationship between events or incidents or other phenomena is easier with interval data than it is with ordinal or nominal data because interval data are more precise. They're all numbers, right? Well, the fact that we have many numbers with interval data can make seeing patterns easier in some cases. If there are too many points, too many variables, and too much "noise" in the data (like background noise in old recordings), it can be much harder. This is the case for all kinds of data, actually.

## Testing for relationships: Interval data

In Chapter 8, we reviewed a series of six questions that guide us through testing for relationships. Just as we did in that chapter for nominal and ordinal data, in this chapter we will together walk through common ways to answer these same questions for interval data. For quick reference, here is the list again, with the statistical language version presented first, with the normal English-language translation in parentheses:

1. Is there an association between the variables?
   *(Is there a consistent pattern in the two sets of data?)*

2. What is the strength of the association?
   *(How strong is the pattern?)*

3. Is one variable having an impact on another? Do you think there may be causality?
   *(Is there a relationship between the two variables?)*

4. What is the direction and nature of that relationship? Which is the dependent and which is the independent variable?)
   *(What kind of relationship is it and what kind of variables are they?)*

5. Is the relationship statistically significant?
   *(Is it statistically significant?)*

6. Is the relationship materially significant?
   *(Does it really matter?)*

## Association and co-movement with interval data

To answer our first two guiding questions, let's start with the idea of *association* as it relates to interval data. As with ordinal or nominal data, association is simply co-movement between two variables. Unlike relationships, with association there is no independent/dependent variable designation because we have not yet established a direction of influence between the variables. We don't know if A influences B, or if B influences A, or if they both influence each other. All we know is that the two variables behave in a similar way: they move together. They do not have to move in a one-for-one pattern (which would actually be a perfect association); however, to show association, if there is a change in one, there must be a change in the other. This is essentially all you are looking for within the data to answer Question 1.

## The correlation coefficient, r

The most common measure used for association in interval data is called **Pearson's correlation coefficient**, denoted by $r$. The computer does the calculation for you, so I will just focus on how to interpret what the computer spits out. Judging the strength of the association is actually easy. The closer the correlation coefficient is to 1 (either negative or positive), the more perfect the association. That is to say, the more perfect the co-movement, the more similar the two data series or variables. If the correlation coefficient is 0, there is no correlation, no similar behavior, no co-movement, and no association. Of course, it is not often that we think there might be a correlation and we come up with a perfect negative 1 or positive 1, or an absolute 0. Usually we are in between. The closer you are to the value of 1 (negative or positive), the stronger the co-movement, and the stronger the association. The closer you are to 0, from either direction, the weaker the co-movement, and the weaker the association. Briefly, the correlation coefficient is all you need to know to answer Question 2 about the strength of the association.

But there is one other consideration. You might want to know the direction of the association. This is where the negative or positive direction comes in. The values of –1 and +1 are the same in terms of strength, as it says just above. The sign of the correlation coefficient represents the nature of the association or possible relationship, whether it is negative or positive. (This will be more important in the next two questions when we consider whether there is a relationship between the variables.) In Chapter 8, we learned a positive association is one in which the values of the two variables increase or decrease together *in the same direction*. As one goes up, the other goes up. A negative association is one in which the values of the two variables increase or decrease together *in opposite directions*. As one goes up, the other goes down. This also means that if one variable changes and there is *no change* in the second variable, then there is no association between the two. In other words, the association between the two variables is 0: no association.

## Spotting patterns in interval data

Luckily, with interval data it is much easier to visually spot similar patterns and see negative and positive patterns, associations, and relationships in the data set than with nominal or ordinal data. In fact, one of the best ways to understand your information and what the data are telling you about association is to plot the values on a **scatter plot** graph, with one data series for one variable along the bottom (the horizontal, or *x*-axis) and the data series for the other variable along the left side (the vertical, or *y*-axis). Each point is plotted on the graph, and you can see if there is a pattern. The way that analysts best understand the association between variables is to fit a line to the plotted data. That is, the computer (thank goodness!) is able to plot a **trendline** along the data points. The line mathematically chooses the path that minimizes its distance from each point as much as possible.

For example, Figure 9–1 is a simple scatter plot showing a positive association. (Remember: We don't know yet whether the pattern constitutes an actual relationship. We are only considering association and co-movement at this point.) You will notice that the line fits the data relatively well: the points are clustered tightly around the line. An analyst would say that the line is a "good fit" to the data.

A negative association looks like the one in Figure 9–2. As with the previous one, the line fits the data well. Both of these graphs show data with a strong association between two variables—so strong, in fact, that the similar positive and negative patterns between each of the variables' data series in each graph would be easily visible without the line. The data are close together, and the pattern going up or down is clear.

If the scatter plot indicated a *perfect* pattern of association rather than only a *similar* pattern, all the data points for each variable would be so tightly clustered as to perfectly align whether the association was negative or positive. In this pattern, the data would all form either a perfectly straight, upward (positively) sloping line or a perfectly straight, downward (negatively) sloping line. Positive sloping or negative sloping, a data pattern in the form of a perfectly straight line mathematically denotes perfect, one-for-one, co-movement of the two variables' data points and creates the perfect (and strongest!) association. The corresponding correlation coefficients would be $+1$ or $-1$, respectively, depending on whether the line sloped positively $(+1)$ or negatively $(-1)$.

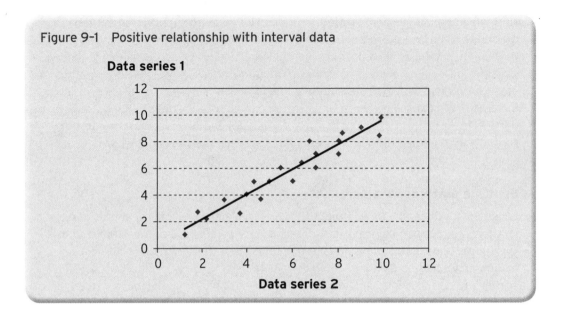

Figure 9-1    Positive relationship with interval data

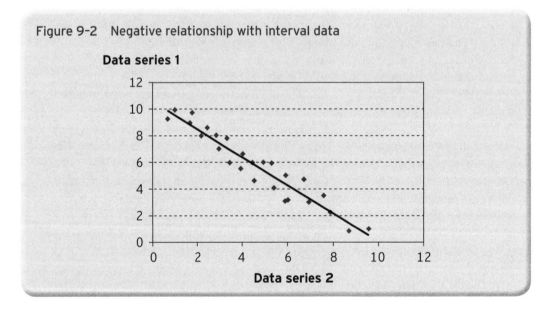

Figure 9-2    Negative relationship with interval data

However, most scatter plots are not so pretty, clear, or perfect. This is one reason that the trendline is a helpful visual tool. If the data are not tightly clustered but instead are spread out and still generally go up in a pattern, the correlation coefficient will be positive but not as close to +1, and the upward slope of the line will not be as steep as in Figure 9–1. The same thing is the case if the pattern is spread out but still generally goes down: the correlation coefficient will be negative but not that close to –1, and the downward slope of the line will not be as steep as in Figure 9–2. Therefore, the pattern of association between the two variables in both scenarios will be weaker since the corresponding correlation coefficients on the scales of 0 to +1 or 0 to –1 will be closer to 0 for both associations.

What kind of association is reflected in Figure 9–3?

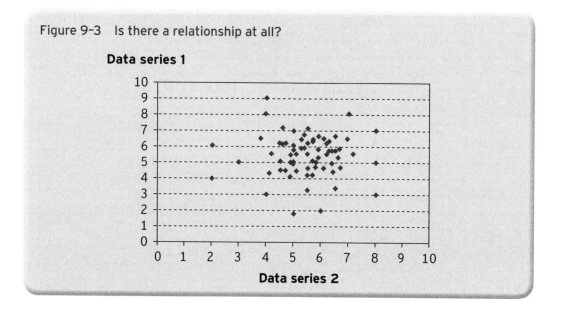

**Figure 9-3   Is there a relationship at all?**

None! No clear pattern of association is present in any particular direction. If you wanted to show that there was an association by fitting a line to the data, you (and the computer) would be hard pressed to decide whether the line should be up and down, side to side, or in any other direction. This is an example of a scatter plot with a correlation coefficient of 0. The line for this graph would actually be perfectly horizontal, denoting no association between the two variables.

We have addressed Guiding Questions 1 and 2 on our list and discussed the concepts of *association* and *co-movement*. Specifically, we now know how to spot when similar patterns within two sets of data denote association between two variables, and we know how to measure the strength of that association. We can now turn our attention to Guiding Questions 3 and 4 of our series.

## Regression: Moving from association to causality with interval data

We are now moving into the world of a **regression**, a concept of statistical analysis that is unique to interval data. Our next two guiding questions will take us first through a discussion of bivariate regression. Then, after establishing a basic understanding, we will look at multivariate regression in the context of Questions 3 and 4.

## Bivariate regression

To answer our next two guiding questions, we must keep some things in mind. Just like with nominal and ordinal data, when we reach this point in our series of guiding questions—that is, we are moving from association to relationship, and then to relationship with causality—we need to identify what we think is the independent variable and what we think is the dependent variable. To start, we stick to just two variables. We'll move to using more in the next section.

Which variable is influencing the other, in our opinion? Thinking in terms of our theoretical models with arrows pointing from one variable to another as in Figures 8–1 and 8–2, we ask, "What do we *think* might be the real direction of the relationship? Which is really influencing which, if at all, in this possible causal relationship?" Working your way through these questions will lead you to your answers to Question 3.

## Causality

However, *always* approach causality with caution! Although we think of ourselves as smart for a species, in the world of research nothing can be absolutely proven. Remember our discussion of probability in Chapter 5? There is *always* a probability that we are wrong in our conclusions, even if that probability is minute. Plus, when we set out to test for causality, we start with assumptions about what is influencing what when we draw our directional arrows from one variable to another in our theoretical models. We essentially guess (sometimes it's an educated guess) about what direction the relationship runs. Does economic growth have an influence on education, or does education have an influence on economic growth? The point is that we have to *pick* the relationship we want to test.

## Approach causality with caution!

Once we've made that selection, we are ready to step into the world of **causality.** Our scatter plot is no longer just two series of data but, rather, one series representing the *independent variable* (always on the *x*-axis) and another representing the *dependent variable* (always on the *y*-axis). We again use the measure of association called the *correlation coefficient*, or *r*, in our estimation for goodness of fit; we understand that a perfect, one-to-one match for *r* denotes perfect association between two variables and equal (one-for-one) co-movement among the data points for both variables. When not a perfect association, it is a value between 0 and +1 or between 0 and –1. The farther from 0, the stronger the association.

## The correlation coefficient squared, $r^2$

But for causality, we don't just accept the value of *r* as we did before; no, that would be too easy! The value of *r* represents *goodness of fit* for *association* purposes. *Causality* is a much bigger deal! We have higher standards! For causality, we use a measure called the $r^2$; it is just that, the correlation coefficient squared. If you square $r$, the resulting value becomes smaller because $r$ is a fraction. It is still a value between 0 and 1 (but not between 0 and –1 because squaring a negative creates a positive), but because it is smaller, we end up with a lower number when we are considering causality; that is what I mean by having a higher standard. For association, a value of $r$ that is 0.50 can be considered fair evidence of association. If squared, to represent causality, the value drops to 0.25. It's lower, but still a measure of goodness of fit. With both association and causality, we use the same term: goodness of fit.

To be technical, $r^2$ represents the amount of **variance** in $y$ (the dependent variable) that can be explained by $x$ (the independent variable) in a bivariate regression. In more simple terms, you might think of it as how closely $y$ is tied to $x$, or how much of an influence $x$ is having on $y$. In a perfect one-to-one, $r^2$ match, if you know $x$, you would automatically know $y$. And you can turn that around: any differences between values of the dependent variable (variance in $y$) would be paralleled by differences in $x$.

> Bivariate regression is about how much of your dependent variable ($y$) can be explained by the independent variable ($x$).

### Describing the nature of the pattern

The huge difference in understanding patterns with interval data as opposed to with nominal or ordinal data is that we can understand if there is a pattern *and* describe the exact nature of that pattern! Think about it: can we fit a line to our scatter plot of data, correct? Yes. We can follow that line and know that at any point for a value of the independent variable, $x$, we can estimate the associated value of the dependent variable, $y$, correct? Yes, which means that once we fit a line to the data, we can get the equation for the line and know the exact nature of the relationship between the two variables! Think back to high school: do you remember the formula for a line?

$$y = mx + b$$

Think hard and you'll remember that $m$ represents the **slope** of the line (rise over run, or change in $y$ over change in $x$), and $b$ represents the **intercept** of the line. We can use our interval data to plot the line.

Let me give you a simple example. On the night of the budget book preparation, when most of the budget staff have to stay late to get everything just right before the council budget retreat the next day, Chuck decides to order pizza for everyone. He gets the local pizzeria special, $5 for a single topping, large. He orders ten pizzas for the staff and looks at the final bill. It is $50. The total cost *depends* on the number of pizzas ordered. As Table 9–1 shows, there is a direct relationship between the number of pizzas ordered and the final bill. It is a positive relationship. As more pizzas are ordered, the total bill goes up.

Plot the line yourself on a scrap of paper, with an *x*-axis and a *y*-axis. In this example, what is the dependent variable? The total bill! Remember: the total cost *depends* on the

**Table 9-1   Pizzas and total bill**

| Number of pizzas | Total bill ($) |
|------------------|----------------|
| 1 | 1 |
| 2 | 10 |
| 3 | 15 |
| 4 | 20 |
| 5 | 25 |

number of pizzas ordered, the independent variable. And what is the exact nature of the relationship? If we plotted the data, we would have a straight line. With a change in *x* (say, one more pizza ordered), there is a corresponding change in *y* of $5. The formula for this line would be the following:

$$y = mx + b.$$

or in our simple example, where there is no "intercept" or b:

$$y = 5x.$$

The slope is positive, so we know that the relationship is positive. As the number of pizzas goes up, the bill goes up. We interpret this by saying (in a deep, slow, academic, and potentially very boring voice), "For every one unit increase of *x*, the slope, also called the **unstandardized beta coefficient**, represents the corresponding change in *y*." *What?* In other words, for every pizza, the bill goes up $5.

But wait! The formula is missing something, isn't it? Where is the intercept? The intercept is where the line would start on (and theoretically intersect) the *y*-axis—the same axis as the dependent variable. For our example, we know from our data that the line goes up, in a perfectly positive, perfectly predictable way. Well, in our case, the intercept is zero, so we won't bother to even put it in the formula. But what if it wasn't zero? What if it was a different value? What would an intercept do in this example? Well, what about the tip? That might tell us. Every good delivery guy or gal deserves a good tip, and of course, the local government offices want to keep up good relations with the local businesses, especially when the budget might include some new business fees. So Chuck always tips $10, regardless of how many pizzas are ordered. With 10 as the intercept, the formula for the line would become the following:

$$y = 5x + 10.$$

It is appropriate here to show you three changes in how we show the equation for a line in regression. First, on the right side of the equation, we put the intercept first. Second, we represent the intercept with the Greek symbol for alpha, $\alpha$. Third, the slope is no longer represented by 'm' but by 'b'. So the standard equation for a line in regression now looks like:

$$y = ? + bx.$$

To go back to our example, the intercept is 10 and the slope of the line is 5. To get the cost of the bill (y), you multiply $5 by the number of pizzas ordered and then add $10. The formula is now:

$$y = 10 + 5x.$$

We know everything we need to predict exactly the pizza bill. In fact, we would say that we could explain all the variance in the bill (the dependent variable, $y$) for every time that Chuck orders pizza by knowing the number of pizzas ordered (the independent variable, $x$) and the tip (the intercept, or starting point). The one independent variable, x, can explain all the variance in the bills: number of pizzas ordered—in this case, 10. So with all the variance explained, the $r^2$ is 1.00! All of the variance, or 100% of the variance, in the pizza bills can be explained by the number of pizzas order and the tip.

I'll return, again, to the value of $r^2$ a few more times, especially when we discuss what the computer produces when we hit the "go" button for a regression analysis.

## Error term

Alas, as we observed before, there are very few perfect relationships in the world. As we've already learned, when we put data into a scatter plot, they usually don't fall into a straight line. It is messier than that. The real world is always messier than abstract mathematics, and now we step beyond the simple equation of a line that we learned in high school. So, how do we deal with that mess, you ask? By scooping it all up and dumping it into a term that we slap on the end of the equation: the **error term** or "**e.**" With the error term, we now have a regression formula, and it looks like this:

$$y = ? + bx + e.$$

Think about the lines that we fit to the data in the plots at the beginning of this chapter. None of the lines fits the data perfectly. There was always some error, some space left between the data points and the line. This is also, why, in the real world, you are never able to perfectly explain all the variance in something. Why does the temperature go up and down? Why does it rain one day and not the next? Are weather forecasters ever accurate? We know a lot about atmosphere, geography, and meteorology, but there is still some aspect of randomness in all science (and life). We can explain a lot but not all. So if $r^2$ is the amount of variation in the dependent variable that we can explain with the independent variable, we would hope for the highest possible value of $r^2$. But we also understand that 1.0 (or 100%) is not a likely result for $r^2$ since it is highly improbable that we can explain all the variation for any phenomenon.

The value of $r^2$ ranges from 0 to 1, representing 0% to 100%. In Figures 9–1 and 9–2, the $r^2$ would be high. But in Figure 9–3, the $r^2$ would be 0, denoting no relationship at all. In this example, one particular line would not be any closer to all the points than any other line. This might be the case of looking at the total pizza bill and plotting it against the hair color of the delivery person. There would be no relationship, no association, and no causality between the two (I hope). The exercise of a bivariate regression is one way to answer Question 4.

## Multivariate regression

Should we look at the big picture? Are we limited to looking at possible relationships, one by one? Luckily, no; and fortunately, computers are amazing. Without computers, I can't imagine being able to move from the case of one independent variable to multiple independent variables, but that's what happens when you move from bivariate regression to **multivariate regression.** As I pointed out earlier, usually models include many factors (many independent variables) that make up the "big picture." Think about economic growth in your community. Is it influenced by just one thing? Of course not. Many things influence economic development: population, climate, crime, employee skills, taxes, culture, incentives, and interest rates, to name a few.

> Multivariate regression lets us look at the big picture, all the variables at once, instead of one by one.

To consider a second independent variable in a regression model, we simply add another *x*-axis. Instead of seeing the scatter plot in two dimensions on a flat page, imagine a three-dimensional space, like the space in the room where you are sitting. Think of points floating in that space, as if you had a balloons floating in different places in the room: some up high, some lower, some to one side, some to another. Imagine drawing a line from a bottom corner across and through the room to the opposite top corner. This is what the computer is doing. It is calculating a line that minimizes the distance from the line to each point (balloon)."

It is too complicated to go into the mathematical details, but this process allows us isolate the impact of each independent variable.

All the rules we discussed for a bivariate regression translate to a multivariate regression:

- The $r^2$ is the same: it is the variation in the dependent variable, the $y$, that can be explained by all the independent variables (all the $x$'s) together.

- The independent variables (each of the $x$'s) have their own slopes with each slope showing the impact that $x$ has on the dependent variable. If that independent variable increases by 1, the value of the slope is the impact on, or change in, the dependent variable. It is the same as in our earlier example of bivariate regression with the pizzas. If Chuck buys one more pizza (the $x$), the cost of the pizza bill ($y$) goes up by \$5. To add in another variable is similar to saying that Chuck is also buying some drinks. For every drink, the bill goes up \$2. You then have a multivariate regression; you have two variables: the number of pizzas and the number of drinks.

- The intercept still shows the starting point (value) for the dependent variable. In our example, regardless of how many pizzas and drinks are bought, Chuck still gives his standard \$10 tip. It is a constant value. It does not change.

- The error term still captures all the messiness that we can't explain through the independent variables, but by the nature of science and life it is still shown in the regression model.

- *This is only for those interested in more advanced methods.*

## Regression assumptions

While regression (bivariate or multivariate) is valuable, it relies on some important assumptions in order for it to work well:

1. *We assume that the model is well specified;* that is, it includes all the variables that are important and no variables that are irrelevant. For example, to explain economic development, you would want to include variables on everything that influences economic development. That would be many arrows on the page!

2. *We assume that the model is linear;* that is, we can fit a line to the data. Most analysts do not go beyond linear regression, but it is possible to fit a curve to data points, too. If you look at a scatter plot of your data and it looks like Figure 9–4, then head to the closest statistician's office and bring donuts. If you tried to fit a straight line to the data, you would get bad results. Remember the donuts. Fresh, hot glazed donuts from a North Carolina based donut shop chain if you are in a hurry.

3. *We assume that there is no* **measurement error.** At the beginning of the book, we discussed validity and reliability in measures and in research design. This is where it is important. Just like with any of our analyses: garbage in, garbage out. If you looked at the extra garlic bread sticks that Chuck ordered and counted them as a \$5 pizza even though they were only \$3.50, your data would be wrong. This would not be good if you were a budget analyst for Chuck and he caught that error. He might start to wonder about your estimates for occupancy tax revenues. This is why I emphasize the importance of good data.

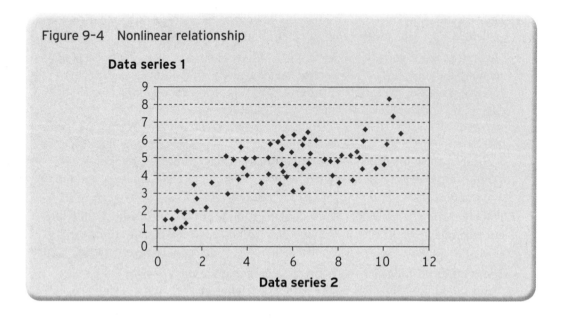

Figure 9-4   Nonlinear relationship

4. *We assume that the model is free of* **multicollinearity.** We want to make sure that we measure things only once. For example, if you were measuring poverty in a community, you might use the variable *average income.* You might also want to use the variable of the *number of children in the school who receive free or reduced price lunches.* But these two things are really measuring the same thing—poverty—so if you include both of them in your model, the computer will not be able to appropriately assess the relationships involved.

5. *We assume that the error term only represents randomness.* We need to know that there is nothing funny going on in the error term, that it truly represents only randomness and not hidden variables or patterns. **There is a lot packed into this assumption,** more than we will discuss here, and assessing the strength of this assumption can be difficult. If you go into the territory of multivariate regression, I would recommend accepting this assumption with grace and crossed fingers or consulting a statistician.

## Statistical and material significance with interval data

You can see that with regression (bivariate or multivariate), more than with any other type of analysis in this book, we can get as close as possible to understanding the relationship between two variables. But we still have our last two guiding questions: (5) Is the relationship statistically significant? and (6) Is the relationship materially significant? In other words, does it really matter?

Both of these guiding questions can be answered with a focus on the regression coefficient, or slope, for each variable. For each variable, the computer has calculated a coefficient for us, correct? Yes. That coefficient is the estimated impact that one unit of change in the independent variable has on the dependent variable, correct? Yes. It is the slope. It is the material impact that the independent variable has on the dependent variable. And with each variable, what do we have? *Confidence intervals* and *confidence levels*! YAHOO!! It all comes back to *t*-scores and *p* values.

Each variable will have a separate *t*-score and an accompanying *p* value. This means we can assess whether the data for that particular independent variable and the dependent variable are in a tight enough pattern for us to be confident there is a relationship between them and not just a random pattern. The *t*-scores and *p* values are interpreted in the same way they have been all along. Usually analysts use the breakpoint confidence level of 95%, with the associated *p* value of .05. Variables with *p* values at or below this level are statistically significant: we can be confident they are having a real impact on our dependent variable. But other independent variables may not show the same level of significance, meaning we have to conclude they do not have an influence on the dependent variable.

## The F-score

The regression model as a whole (multivariate) has a measure of statistical significance, too. It is called the **F-score.** I know, I know, you are fed up with the alphabet soup. But there is hope! The F-score represents the statistical significance of the entire model. It also has a *p* value associated with it, which is interpreted in exactly the same way. Just keep looking for the low, low *p* values. If any individual variable is statistically significant (as shown by a low *p* value), the F-score should be statistically significant (as shown by a low *p* value). We look for *p* values that fit the benchmark values I discussed earlier in the book: .10 (90% confidence), .05 (95% confidence), and .001 (99.9% confidence). Those are the models and variables on which to focus. If none of the independent variables are statistically significant (not reaching even the lowest-benchmark value of 90%), the F-score will not be statistically significant. And if something (model or variable) is not statistically significant, we can't say the values are anything other than random. We got nuthin'.

It bears repeating: multivariate regression allows us to understand

1. The individual impacts that each independent variable has on the dependent variable (*y*) through the statistical significance measures (the *t*-scores and *p* values with each variable) and the unstandardized beta coefficients (the slopes, or material impacts)

2. The statistical significance and explanatory power of the model as a whole (the *p* value associated with the model F-score and the model *r²*).

There are many nuances to using and interpreting regression. I have not covered all the assumptions, all the various tests and numbers that would be on a printout, or when to choose this value over some other value when reporting results. Even if I did, you would not remember those rules when you were actually faced with data and an audience demanding help, such as a citizen group or the council or board. The explanation in this chapter is to help you understand that a sophisticated tool exists that can determine if there is a relationship between two things (e.g., the number of pizzas and the bill, or between tax breaks and economic growth). However, this tool can also help us understand the exact nature of that relationship: we know how much the bill will go up with each additional pizza, and how much the economy will grow with a new tax break.

## Chuck put the phone down and was quiet for a little bit. He stood

up, opened the door to his office, and sat back down. It was after hours, and no one else was around. He sometimes stayed late on Tuesdays, cleaning up things that the council had asked him to do. He hated to let those kinds of things sit for a couple of days because you never knew what else would come up. And if nothing happened, well, there was the golf game and pizza to enjoy.

But would there be something like that in Scotts Bluff, which had just asked him to become one of the final four candidates for its manager? Would there be guys like Will and Rex? And what about Yvette? They had been on the library board together for a year, and he really enjoyed the meetings—and not because of the thrill of deciding on new shelving or how to raise money to refurbish the elevator. He realized he enjoyed seeing her each week. The last couple of meetings, they had even gotten coffee afterward to talk about books they liked and gossip about the retiring librarian.

Still, it was appealing. Scotts Bluff was a much bigger city than Council Top, and it was a natural thing for a manager to be around for a couple of years and then move on. At first, he was excited: the chance to be a manager in a place with a larger staff, larger budget! And larger issues, of course. Plus, it had done a lot for his ego. The recruiter said the council in Scotts Bluff had heard about the advances in Council Top: steady growth, high citizen satisfaction, the ability to use information to defuse contentious issues, and good communication with the press and community groups.

Now he had to commit to participate in an assessment process. He would have to be public about the search and the chance that he would leave. If he went for it but didn't get the job, he knew that he would have burned bridges and that his time in Council Top would be short, even if everything was civil and they were supportive. No one likes to be considered second best or a stepping-stone.

If he did leave, he would suggest that Nina apply for his position. She had developed an excellent reputation with the council. Her position had been elevated to assistant manager for management and budget. The council members loved her. When she discussed an issue, she spoke as though she knew all aspects of the issue, and given them equal consideration. Rather than jump to conclusions, she gathered information and questioned every assumption, even if it took some time. She was slow to draw conclusions, but when she made a recommendation, it was firm. And she had clearly been able to hire and bring on talented staff. Maria had been working full time as assistant manager for special projects for over a year, and the other former intern, Max, was filling in for a budget analyst who was out on family leave and not likely to return. He was as good as Nina was and Maria had been, if not better.

The city would be safe.

Chuck flipped open his phone, and then stopped and closed it. He opened it once more and punched in a number.

"Hello, Yvette? This is Chuck. I've been meaning to ask you something for awhile. Would you like to go to a movie this weekend?"

## Review questions

1. What is a measure of association?
2. How would you interpret a correlation coefficient of 0?
3. Why can't you use regression to try to understand the relationship between the following variables?
   a. The influence of a person's sex on his or her hair color
   b. The influence of whether someone smokes on the kind of car she or he drives
4. A regression line is sometimes called the "best fit." What do you think this means?
5. What is a regression coefficient?
6. How would the regression equation for Table 9–1 change if you always gave the pizza delivery person a $5 tip?
7. What is the difference between a bivariate regression and a multivariate regression?
8. What does $r^2$ measure?
9. If you performed a regression analysis, looking at the influence of temperature and rain on crop yields (e.g., how many bushels of corn are produced per acre), how would you interpret an $r^2$ value of 0.85?
10. A person's memory improves as he or she grows from a child to an adult, but then it gets worse again with age. Could linear regression be used with this example to show the relationship between age and memory? Explain why or why not.

# Glossary

**Association:** Having a similar pattern. Measures of association indicate if data for two variables have similar patterns. Association is measured in terms of being weak (close to zero) or strong (close to one).

**Average:** The mean. The sum of all observations in the data set divided by the number of observations.

**Bimodal distribution:** A distribution that has two distinct groupings in the data.

**Categorical data:** Nominal data. Data that describe a category or group without numerical or ranking value. Gender, region, and ethnic group are examples of categorical data.

**Causal relationship:** A relationship where one variable has an impact or influence on another. In other words, a relationship where one variable causes the other to some greater or lesser extent.

**Chi square:** A value produced as a test of a statistically significant relationship between nominal and/or ordinal data. It represents the difference between the actual distribution of data in a contingency table and the distribution that would occur if no relationship existed between the two variables.

**Clean the data:** To prepare data for analysis by eliminating or correcting problems such as typographical errors or mislabeled data and examining outliers or data points that seem unusual.

**Conditional probability:** A probability of an event or condition that depends on, or is conditional on, the probability of a prior event or condition. For example, if your data set were all citizens in a town, the probability of owning a car, given the citizen lived in the suburbs, would be a conditional probability. The first probability is calculated as the number of people living in the suburbs divided by the number of all citizens. The second, or conditional, probability is the number of people owning a car divided by the number of people who live in the suburbs.

**Confidence (level of):** The standard used by the researcher for drawing conclusions for a population from a study using sample data. For example, a 95% confidence level means the researcher can be confident that 19 out of 20 times, the results from our analysis of sample data are correct. There is only a 1 out of 20 (or 5%) chance that the conclusions we draw are incorrect.

**Confidence interval:** Margin of error around a statistical estimate. The confidence interval can be wider or narrower depending on the level of confidence you are using as your standard. For example, you can use statistics to estimate average income. Your result, your estimated average income, will have a lower and higher bracket—this is the confidence interval. As a researcher you are 90, 95, or 99.9% confident the true value lies within those brackets.

**Confidence level:** The level of confidence you choose to use as a researcher. Commonly used confidence levels are 90, 95, and 99.9%. To be 90% confident in your result requires less evidence than to be 99.9% confident. If you are using inferential statistics, a 90% confidence level allows for a 10% chance your conclusions are wrong.

**Contingency table:** Also called a cross tabulation or "cross-tabs." A table of nominal and/or ordinal data organized in rows and columns used to see how the data are distributed across groups. Commonly, a contingency table is a 3x3 table. When used to explore relationships between variables, the proposed independent variable is shown in the columns and the dependent variable is shown in the rows. The outer column and row show totals.

**Cross-sectional data**: Data that are from a single point in time. It is similar to seeing a cross-section of information or a snapshot. Examples of cross sectional data would be average income in 2011 by state, percentage of women employees in different types of industry in 2012, or number of 2013 graduates in different schools in a large school system.

**Data:** Information in any form that can be photographs, stories, focus group discussions, numbers, etc.

**Data distribution:** How data are distributed or dispersed across another variable, such as value, years, geographic locations, size or organizations. For example, if we wish to know how many or what percent of students received As, Bs, Cs, Ds, and Fs in a course, we are asking for the distribution of grades in the course.

**Data points:** Each observation in a data set. Usually the term is used to help us "visually" see the distribution of the data.

**Data series:** A series of data on a single variable. A stream or list of data, such as 3, 7, 5, 10, 13.

**Data set:** Multiple series of data. In other words, a stream or list of data for more than one variable.

**Dependent variable:** When exploring a directional or causal relationship between two variables, the dependent variable is the one being influenced by something else, called the independent variable. In other words, a researcher is testing the hypothesis that the value of the dependent variable depends on other, independent variable(s). For example, a researcher might want to test if the amount of job training influences job performance. Job performance would be the dependent variable since you are looking on whether or not performance *depends* on the amount of training. *See also* independent variable.

**Descriptive statistics:** Information that describes the data for a variable. For example, the mean, median, and mode, and highest and lowest value are all descriptive statistics.

**Estimate**: Best guess based on data in the analysis.

**Event:** Something that happens or a characteristic being considered. "Event" is a term often used in probability, especially in conditional probabilities. Conditional probability requires two "events" that are considered in order. For example, the phrase "the probability of being sick given you are at the doctor's office" requires two events. The first "event" is being at the doctor's office. The second "event" is whether or not you are sick.

**Frequency:** A count. Frequencies of the data are counts for each value in a data set. For example, if you want frequencies of a data set of ages of students in a classroom, the result could be 5 students under 20, 7 students aged 21 to 30, 5 students aged 31 to 40, and 2 students aged 40 and over. The count of data observations in each category is a frequency.

**Frequency distribution:** The distribution of the frequencies for each value of a variable. The frequency distribution of the data set of ages of students in a classroom would be considering all the frequencies as a group and arranging them in some order.

**Histogram:** A graph showing a frequency distribution.

**Independent variable:** When exploring a directional or causal relationship between two variables, the independent variable is the one influencing something else, called the dependent variable. In other words, a researcher is testing the hypothesis that the value of the dependent variable depends on other, independent variable(s). For example, a researcher might want to test if the amount of job training influences job performance. Job performance would be the dependent variable since you are looking on whether or not performance *depends* on the amount of training. *See also* dependent variable.

**Inferential statistics:** In contrast to descriptive statistics, which describes only the data at hand, inferential statistics allows us to infer something from a sample to a larger population. That is, we are using inferential statistics to draw a conclusion that can be applied beyond the bounds of the data at hand.

**Interquartile range:** The range between the upper and lower value of the middle 50% of observations in a data series. Imagine you separate all of the observations in your data set into 4 equal parts. The middle 2 parts represent the middle 50% of the observations. The interquartile range is the distance between the value at the bottom of that middle 50% and the value at the top of the middle 50%.

**Interval data:** Data that have an equal and measurable distance between points. In other words, there is an equal interval between the values. The numbers 1, 2, 3, and 4 are interval data. So are 5%, 6%, and 7%; and so are 21 years old, 54 years old, and 3 years old. Usually any data with numbers are interval data.

**Joint probability:** The probability of two things happening or existing at once. For example, the probability of a student in a classroom having brown hair *and* having a job is a joint probability. Another example would be the probability of being a part-time *and* permanent employee. Finally, the probability of having a car accident while texting is a joint probability. It is the probability of these two things being done by a driver out of all drivers. You should note this is not the same as the probability of having an accident *given* that you are texting. This latter example is the probability of a single person, from the group of people who are texting, having an accident. This latter example is a conditional probability.

**Longitudinal data** or **longitudinal study:** Data collected or a study conducted over time. An example would be a study that tracked participation in special emergency management training over ten years.

**Margin of error:** Also referred to standard error. When an analyst uses sample data to estimate a value, such as average pay, she knows her estimate is likely to be a little too low or a little too high. The margin of error is the lower and upper bounds within which the analyst is confident the true value lies. For example, when estimating average pay rates, an analyst may get a value of $37,000 with a margin of error of plus or minus $3,000. The margin of error depends on how confident you want to be that the "bookends" you use includes the true value. We usually use the 95% confidence level. That means the analyst is 95% confident the true value of average pay is somewhere between $34,000 and $40,000.

**Material significance:** Whether or not the estimated impact of one variable on another is large enough to be important for the question at hand. For example, the impact of an additional year of education on income might be $1,000—large enough to make a material difference for most people. If the impact were only $5, the impact would not be materially significant. Material significance has to be determined by the context of the question and is a subjective judgment.

**Mean:** The average. The mean is obtained by adding up (summing) all the values in a data set and then dividing the sum by the *number* of values. If you added

5 values in a data set together, getting a sum of 60, you would divide by 5. The average value in that data set is 12.

**Measures of central tendency:** Measures that tell you where the bulk of the values in your data set lie. Where does the center of the data tend to be? High? Low? In the middle? There are three measures of central tendency: the mean (see above), median (the middle value), and mode (the most common value).

**Measures of dispersion:** Measures that tell you how spread out the data are. Are the data higher dispersed, stretched out from the mean in a higher or lower way, or in both directions? Or narrowly dispersed or tightly clustered around the mean? The most common measures of dispersion are the range and standard deviation. They can only be interpreted when combined with the mean to put it in context. For example, say you have a data set of response times for 911 calls and the average is 3 minutes. If the spread of the data is from 2 minutes 45 seconds to 3 minutes 15 seconds, you might consider the data to be tightly clustered around the mean. If the spread of the data is from 30 seconds to 9 minutes, you might consider the data to be widely spread out.

**Median:** The middle value in a data set; the value where half of the observations are above and half of the observations are below. Of course, this works easily only when there are an odd number of observations. When there is an even number of observations, the median is the mid-point between the middle two values (one would add the two middle values together and divide by two.)

**Mode:** The most common value in a data set. For example, in a data set of values of number of years of education for a randomly selected group of citizens, if the most people said is 12 (high school), the mode value would be 12—even if the overall average would be higher or lower.

**Moving average:** Sometimes data over time moves up and down year to year, creating a jagged line on a graph. In an effort to smooth the jagged line, we can transform each point by turning it into the average of three numbers; the value for the point before, the point itself, and the point after. When graphed, the resulting new data will be a smoothed out version of the original jagged line. This is called taking a moving average. A moving average can be calculated for 3 months, 3 years, 5 years, 10 years, or any other amount of time. The more points used to make the moving average, the smoother the resulting line will be when graphed.

**Negative skew:** In a data distribution, you can have an outlier to one side or the other. A distribution with a negative skew is where there are outliers to the left, creating an image of the bulk of data to the right and a "tail" stretching out to the left. You can also recognize a negative skew when the mean (average) of a data set is lower than the median (middle value). The outliers to the left (usually lower values) are pulling the mean away from the median to the left.

**Nominal data:** Data that do not have a measured/measurable value (called interval data) or even a relative value (called ordinal data). Nominal data are categories like gender (female or male), region (north, south, east, or west), or taste (sweet, sour, savory). Nominal data are also called categorical data.

**Normal curve:** A description of data that fall in a normal distribution (see next entry). It represents the curved, bell-shaped line that could be drawn across the top of a normal distribution. Normal curves can also be described as bell curves.

**Normal distribution:** A distribution of data that forms a bell shaped curve. A normal distribution is symmetric, meaning the shape on one side of the distribution mirrors the other side—the sides are equal. The definition of a normal distribution is one where the mean, median, and mode are exactly the same. If the data fall into a normal distribution we can say the data are "normal," "normally distributed," or we have "normality." Normal distributions are very important to statistics because many of the analytical tools we use ($z$-scores, $t$-tests, regression) are based on the assumption of normality. *See discussion of central limit theorem on page 62.*

**Observation:** A case or one unit of the things you are measuring. For example, in a study of cities, Minneapolis would be one observation. Atlanta would be a second observation.

**Ordinal data:** Data that do not have a measured/measurable value (called interval data) but instead a relative value. An example of ordinal data is "poor," "fair," and "excellent" or "unsatisfied," "satisfied," and "very satisfied."

**Outcome:** An objective, perhaps the ultimate goal or purpose of an action. It is often used in performance measurement. An objective for a financial education course for potential home owners might be the reduction and eventual elimination of home foreclosures.

**Outlier:** A value that is an uncommon extreme in the context of a data set. The income level of Bill Gates, the co-founder of Microsoft, would be an outlier in a sample of household incomes in the state of Washington.

***p* value:** The probability that a pattern in or distribution of data could occur by simple random chance. *P* values are used to measure statistical significance in inferential statistics. A *p* value of .05 says there is only a 5% chance the data distribution seen in the data set in question could be the result of simple, random chance. Alternatively, we would say that we were 95% confident (1.0 minus .05 or 100% minus 5%) that the data distribution we see is NOT random.

**Panel data:** Data that are a combination of cross sectional and time series (i.e., across geography, people, organizations, and over time). An example of panel data would be the educational achievement scores of a group of children in a special education program over 10 years.

**Percentage distribution:** Rather than showing the distribution of data in terms of the values of observation, you can show the distribution of data in terms of percentage of the total number of observations. For example, in an election with 7 republican candidates jockeying for the position as the party nominee, you could show what share, or percentage, of the republican voters support each candidate. This is almost always represented as a percentage distribution.

**Perfect relationship:** A relationship where you can see perfectly predictable co-movement between two data series. For example, if there is a one unit increase in one data series, there would be a predictable, set movement of the values in the other data series. If on Monday nights a large pizza from Anna Maria's Pizza Parlor in Carrboro costs $7 (not tax, tips, or other orders), the ultimate bill would perfectly align. For each pizza, the bill goes up $7. If you reduce the number of pizzas ordered, the bill goes down $7. A perfect relationship can be positive (the two series move in the same direction, like the number of pizzas and the bill) or negative (the two series move in an inverse or negative way, like for every additional person wearing a UNC tee shirt to the pizza parlor the bill goes down 10%).

**Population:** All possible observations in a group. For example, if you sent a survey to all citizens of Joplin, Missouri, you would be surveying the population. There are 117 school districts in North Carolina. If you gathered data on school enrollment of non-English-speaking children from all 117 schools, you would have the population of data.

**Positive skew:** In a data distribution, you can have an outlier to one side or the other. A distribution with a positive skew is where there are outliers to the right, creating an image of the bulk of data to the left and a "tail" stretching out to the right. You can also recognize a positive skew when the mean (average) of a data set is higher than the median (middle value). The outliers to the right (usually higher values) are pulling the mean away from the median to the right.

**Presample:** As a verb, before conducting a study, taking a small portion of the data and analyzing it before conducting the regular data-gathering portion of the research design. As a noun, it is the observations included in that small portion. For example, when conducting a citizen survey, you should take a presample of 10 or 15 citizens and ask them to take the survey in advance so you can correct any mistakes before the full survey is conducted.

**Probability:** Probability is a measure of how often one outcome tends to happen when you consider all the possible outcomes that could happen. It is a percentage or a rate or "chance of" or likelihood. For example, if you picked 10 days at random in Seattle, 4 of those days would have rain. To find the probability of something happening, you have to have information on past patterns—in this case, of the weather every day in the past $x$ years in Seattle—and how many of those days were rainy and how many were sunny (assuming there are only two options, rainy or sunny). If 40% of the days were rainy, we have the probability of rain in the future. It is important to remember that probabilities are predictions, and like any prediction (or guess), whether educated with past data or not, can be wrong.

**Quartiles:** The four quarters of the data. You can break your observations into the highest 25% of observations (or quartile), the next highest 25%, the next lower 25%, and finally the lowest 25% (or quartile).

**Random data set:** When a sample of data are selected in a way such that each person or thing has an *equal chance* of being chosen. If there is any bias in the way data are selected, the resulting data are not random.

**Randomness:** The benefit that comes with having a randomly selected dataset. True randomness means any differences that exist in a population are very likely to show up in a sample in about the same proportion. Another way to think about it is that the probability of a particular characteristic of the data showing up would be the same for each observation. For example, if you wanted to survey people about healthy life habits, and 20% of the overall population smokes, randomness says that about 20% of the sample will probably smoke. Any outside factors are equally likely to influence anyone in a control or in an experimental group. The bottom line is that randomness protects against bias and threats to validity. Because everyone has the same chance of having a characteristic that exists in the population, you won't have a control group or experimental group that is purposely biased in one way or another. One group will not have all the smokers while the other one will not have all non-smokers (at least, it's highly unlikely that you could randomly select a control and experimental group with that breakdown. All differences (except for the one we are focused on, like an experimental drug that goes just to the experimental group) should be equally distributed across both control and experimental groups. We don't need to worry about either group being biased in one direction or another on any other characteristic.

**Range:** The lowest to highest value in a data set. Sometimes it is reported as the value of the highest observation minus the lowest observation. For example, a study of the average number of fire calls per capita in Iowa cities in FY 2010 might include a range of 0.3 fire calls per capita in Mason City to 1.5 fires in Coralville. The range is 0.3 to 1.5, or 1.2.

**Response rate:** You can get response rates in different ways. The most common one is the percent of *usable* responses of the total surveys distributed (as opposed to just responses—some completed surveys may need to be thrown out because of major problems such as someone filling it out under the alias of their favorite TV character. These responses should not be counted in the responses). In addition, you can have responses rates for individual questions because people sometimes skip questions. Only the overall response rate is normally reported in the main text of a study.

**Sample:** A subset of the population; a small portion of a much larger group. For example, surveying only 2,000 people of the entire population of the United States (over 300 million) would be taking a sample.

**Sample error:** The error you get when you try to use a sample to estimate a value for a population. For example, if trying to measure average income of working adults in Oklahoma, you might use a random sample of 2,000 people across the state. You would get a sample average. This average would likely not exactly match the value you would get it if you were able to ask the same question of every working adult in the entire state—the "true" value. The difference between the true value and the sample value is referred to as the sample average. As everything with sample, though, the sample error is estimated. Could there be a sample error error? Possibly.

**Sampling:** The process of studying a sub-set rather than everyone or everything in the population. It makes research a lot easier, but it also means you are always dealing with estimates, which brings its own problems, such as sample error. *See also* sample error.

**Sensitivity analysis:** Testing your analysis by changing some of the assumptions or values used. For example, if estimating costs of a wedding in Iowa in May, you might get a range of estimates depending on if it rains, snows, is sunny and perfect, or extremely hot and muggy ending with a severe thunderstorm. In public administration research, you should vary some of your assumptions as well—how would future growth estimates be impacted by higher than expected inflation? Lower than expected population growth? If sensitivity analysis shows all positive (or all negative) results even when you vary assumptions, than you have a strong conclusion. If your results change when you vary assumptions, your results are not very strong—they can't stand up under sensitivity analysis.

**Skewed:** Data or a distribution can be skewed, meaning the data are unevenly distributed, not in a normal, bell-shape curve, or an even, flat line. Generally, it means the bulk of the data lie to the upper or lower part of the range, with a "tail" of data to one side or the other. *See* positive skew *or* negative skew.

**Smoothing the data:** The process of transforming the data in such a way as to take out sharp changes, peaks and valleys, or a jagged path. Generally, you smooth the data to bring attention to the overall, long-term pattern, downplaying the point to point changes. *See* moving average.

**Standard deviation:** Officially, it is the square root of the average squared distance of each point to the mean in a data set. In simpler terms, standard deviation is a measure of dispersion in a data set. It gives you a sense of width of the data set, also in the context of the value of the mean. Are there very high values compared to the mean? Very low values? If so, the standard deviation will be high relative to the value of the mean. If all the data are tightly clustered around the mean, the standard deviation is small relative to the mean. Using the standard deviation in most statistical calculations can tell you so much about what the data look like, just in one number.

**Standardize:** To make patterns in data comparable even when the different series are in different units. For example, in a multiple regression, the results include unstandardized coefficients and standardized coefficients. Only standardized coefficients can be used to compare the *relative* impact of the variables included in a model.

**Statistical independence:** Two "events" are statistically independent if the probability of one is the same as the probability of that one *given* the other. First, an event simply means that something happens or exists. Having black hair can be considered an "event." So can graduating from college, owning a yellow car, or dying from cancer. To be statistically independent means that two events are not related, and knowing the probability of one event does not help you in predicting the probability of the other event in any way. For example, if I were to pick a person from your extended family at random, what is the probability of that person being female? We could figure that out by knowing the number of females versus males in the total population of your extended family. The more females, the higher the likelihood, or probability, that if I chose a person at random she would be female. Now let's add in a second "event"—the probability of choosing someone who likes vanilla ice cream. Would knowing if someone chosen randomly from your extended family likes vanilla ice cream help me in predicting whether or not that person was female? No (or at least I don't think there is any connection between liking ice cream and gender). In this case, we would say gender and attitude toward vanilla ice cream are statistically independent. The text includes a more complete discussion of how this is proved with actual probabilities.

**Statistical significance:** Statistical significance is the idea that something—two "events" (*see* statistical independence) or a pattern between two series of data—is so unusual that we cannot believe it is occurring simply due to random chance. If the chance of this happening due to random chance is extremely small, it is statistically improbable. Of course, if this is improbable, the chance of the event happening for some particular reason, a reason we are exploring in our work, increases. For both of these reasons, the low likelihood a pattern or event happening due to random forces and the connected high likelihood it happens due to an identified reason, we call the results of our analysis statistically significant. *See the text for a full explanation.*

**Stratified sampling:** Sometimes when you want to select a sample of data from a population, you want to make sure a particular group or type of data is included. For example, let's say you wanted to take a sample of the students at a university.

Every student would have an equal probability of being included in the sample. We would expect that while there would be around the same number of freshmen, sophomores, juniors and seniors in the sample (assuming there is around the number in each class in the population), there is always the chance that there would be a lot more of one class than another. Remember, random selection can be random, and there is always a change of an uneven sample. If you want to *ensure* an equal number of students from each class in the sample, you would stratify, or break, your sample into four groups, and choose an equal number from each class.

**Time series:** Data that are recorded over time, such as annual GDP growth rates or city population, daily temperatures, or annual flood levels. A time-series data set is made up of data all of which are recorded over time.

*t*-**score:** In general, *t*-score is the number of standard errors from a point to the mean of a distribution of data. It could also be the number of standard errors between the means of two samples of data. A *t*-score is simply a measure to understand the distance between two points, all in the context of the mean and standard deviation of the data set(s) you are using. It is used in statistics as a measure of whether or not the distance between the two points is small or large. If the distance is two standard errors or greater, or has a *t*-score of 2, the difference between those two values is considered statistically significant. *See* statistical significance.

*t*-**test:** A t-test is a statistical test of two points to determine the T-score. It is most often used to understand if two samples are statistically significantly different. For example, one could be testing to see if response times for unionized police departments are statistically significantly different from response times for non-unionized police departments.

**Type I error:** Where a true null hypothesis is incorrectly rejected. In regular terms, a Type I error occurs when a researcher concludes he or she has a significant result, or that something is going on, a connection or relationship exists, when in reality *there is nothing going on and no connection or relationship exists.* We tend to discuss this in the context of having a high or low bar for statistical significance. If we set the bar low, requiring the $p$ value or probability of the result being due to random chance to be relatively high, such as 10% (.10), we may "find" a statistically significant result when one doesn't exist.

**Type II error:** Where a false null hypothesis is incorrectly accepted. In regular terms, a Type II error occurs when a researcher concludes he or she does not have a significant result, or that nothing is going on, no connection or relationship exists, when in reality there *is something going on, there is a connection or a relationship does exist.* We tend to discuss this in the context of having a high or low bar for statistical significance. If we set the bar extremely high, requiring the $p$ value or probability of the result being due to random chance to be relatively low, such as 0.10% (.001), we may ignore a statistically significant result when one really does exist.

**Unit of analysis:** The level of data you have from most detailed to most broad. You could also think of it as the type of data you are gathering. For example, a study of educational achievement could be done at the student, classroom, school, district, state, or national level. Each of these levels represents a different unit of analysis. You can always think of the data you actually have in hand—if you have lots of teacher interviews, the data are at the teacher, or individual person, unit of analysis. If you have average SAT scores from all high schools in the state, the unit of analysis is the high school. Knowing what unit of analysis you have is important because other, possibly related data should be at the same unit. For example, with a study of SAT scores at the school unit of analysis, you would want to understand the percentage of children on free and reduced price lunch (a measure of poverty) at the school or the average classroom size in the school.

**Variable:** Something that varies! Seriously—a variable can be anything that has different values or categories, such as gender, time, shape, texture, color, price, height, depth, smell, size, rivers, wheels, or number of moons (when speaking of planets in our solar system). If something does not vary *in your data set*, it cannot serve as a variable *in your data set*. For example, if you surveyed all students in a high school class and they were all seniors, year in school would not be a variable. All students would be seniors—there is no variability.

**Weighted data:** All data are considered equal unless you weight some more than others. Weighting a value or part of your data set makes those observations more important, or has a heavier weight, relative to the others. If you are doing a study of satisfaction with police services, you may want to place more value on comments from individuals who have had personal contact with an officer in the past year. You would weight those values more heavily than others. Weighting can be actually changing a number to have a higher value or impact in the statistical analysis, or you can just try to consider the information in a different way, subjectively, in your overall research conclusions.

# Index

**Statistics for Public Administration:**
**Practical Uses for Better Decision Making**

Text type
Interstate, ITC Slimbach

Printing and binding
United Book Press, Inc., Baltimore, MD

Design
Charles Mountain,
ICMA, Washington, D.C.